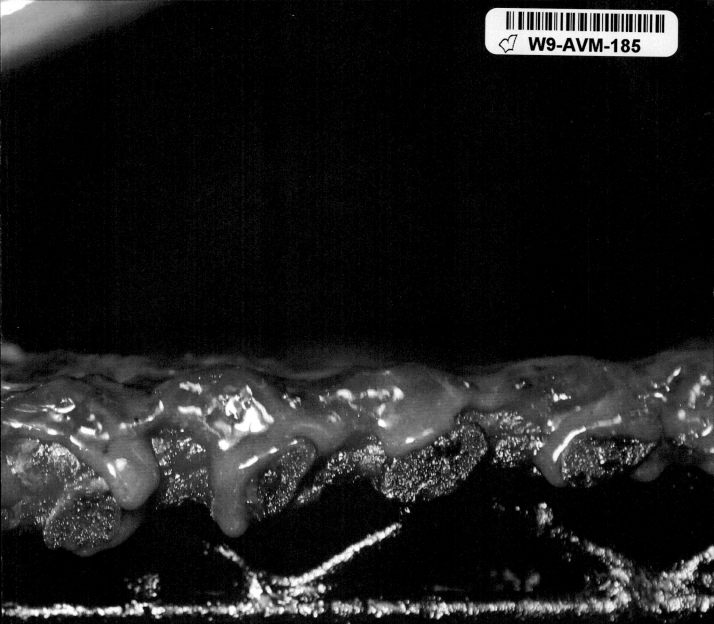

PRAISE
THE LARD

PRAISE
THE LARD

RECIPES AND REVELATIONS

FROM A

LEGENDARY LIFE

IN BARBECUE

MIKE MILLS and AMY MILLS

Photographs by
KEN GOODMAN

A Rux Martin Book
Houghton Mifflin Harcourt
Boston • New York • 2017

Copyright © 2017 by Mike Mills and Amy Mills
Photographs © 2017 by Ken Goodman
Photographs on front endpaper and pages 22 and
326 by David Grunfeld
Brown wood image: Sutichak Yachiangkham/123RF
White wood image: Algirdas Urbonavicius/123RF

For information about permission to
reproduce selections from this book, write to
trade.permissions@hmhco.com or to Permissions,
Houghton Mifflin Harcourt Publishing Company,
3 Park Avenue, 19th Floor, New York, New York 10016.

www.hmhco.com

Library of Congress Cataloging-in-Publication Data
Names: Mills, Mike, date, author. | Tunnicliffe, Amy Mills,
author. | Goodman, Ken (Photographer), photographer.
Title: Praise the lard : recipes and revelations from a
legendary life in barbecue / Mike Mills and Amy Mills ;
photographs by Ken Goodman. Description: Boston :
Houghton Mifflin Harcourt, 2017. | "A Rux Martin Book."
Identifiers: LCCN 2016051671 (print) | LCCN 2016054384
(ebook) | ISBN 9780544702493 (paper over board) |
ISBN 9780544702509 (ebook) Subjects: LCSH: Barbecuing. |
LCGFT: Cookbooks. Classification: LCC TX840.B3 M545
2017 (print) | LCC TX840.B3 (ebook) | DDC 641.7/6—dc23
LC record available at https://lccn.loc.gov/2016051671

Book design by Toni Tajima
Food styling by Amy Mills and Lisa Donovan
Cocktail styling by RH Weaver
Prop styling by Amy Mills and Lisa Donovan

Printed in China
SCP 10 9 8 7 6 5 4 3 2 1

There's something like a line of gold thread running
through a man's words when he talks to his daughter,
and gradually over the years it gets to be long enough
for you to pick up in your hands and weave into
a cloth that feels like love itself.

—**John Gregory Brown**

CONTENTS

WELCOME TO THE
CHURCH OF BARBECUE
#17ST
the Warehouse
17th Street
CATERING ★ EVENTS
618-684-8902
17thstreetbbq.com
BARBECUE

THE GOSPEL ACCORDING TO 17TH STREET

BARBECUE HAS been important to our family, but I never dreamed it would consume my life. And I certainly never set out to get the kind of attention and acclaim that our food has received the world over. Every day for the past thirty-some years, I've focused on three things: cooking consistently good barbecue, helping the people who work for me have a better life, and providing for my own family.

In the beginning, all I wanted was to create the kind of gathering place where I'd want to hang out, a place where people would feel good and warm, as if they were in my home, and where they could talk over a couple of cold beers and maybe enjoy a decent meal—the kind of comforting dishes my family loved, with smoked meats and ribs as a special one or two days a week. I called the place 17th Street Bar & Grill, and before long, it became the spot to be in our tiny city of Murphysboro, Illinois.

I had no idea how much 17th Street would mean to people, or how much hometown pride we would eventually inspire. Two years after opening the restaurant, some friends and I founded Murphysboro's own barbecue cook-off to bring some commerce and attention to our town. Now known as Praise the Lard, the cook-off is in its third decade. We formed our own team—Apple City Barbecue, named after our town's CB radio handle and the area's abundant apple orchards. We quickly became the winningest team on the national barbecue circuit, and the pride of Murphysboro. Parades were thrown to celebrate our victories, and friends and neighbors lined the streets to cheer us on. Regional media covered our comings and goings. Then there was the time President Bill Clinton came to Southern Illinois to give a speech and the Secret Service gave me top security clearance so I could board Air Force One to bring the president some of our ribs and other barbecue fixin's.

In 1990, we won our first World Champion and Grand World Champion titles at Memphis in May, the Super Bowl of barbecue competitions, and a "Home of the Apple City Barbecue Team" sign went up at the Murphysboro city limits. To this day, people flock from all over to compete in our cook-off, serve as judges and volunteers, and, of course, eat our food at 17th Street. Barbecue put Murphysboro (population 7,894) on the map.

AND THAT WAS ALL IN THE FIRST DECADE. In 2002, I helped Danny Meyer open his barbecue restaurant, Blue Smoke, in New York City, and the year after, I helped him and the Blue Smoke team found the Big Apple Barbecue Block Party, Manhattan's very own barbecue festival. In 2005, Amy and I published our first book, and we were showered with all kinds of attention. We appeared on *Regis and Kelly*. *Bon Appétit* anointed our ribs "Best in America," and the Food Network came calling. I remember thinking to myself, "This is it, right here. Barbecue has hit its peak in popularity."

Boy, was I wrong. Interest in barbecue has soared even higher since then and has yet to taper off, because barbecue is about so much more than just the food. Barbecue is America's original comfort food: It feeds the soul. Magic happens around the fire. Time stands still. People talk and share stories, ideas, hopes, dreams. Tending a pit is intentional and methodical, slow and steady, stoked by conversation or contemplation. You can taste that in the meat.

Every year at the Big Apple Barbecue Block Party, I watch these New Yorkers, racing up and down the sidewalks, with their high heels clacking, walking their dogs—it seems like everybody has a dog, and those dogs, they have outfits and little shoes, too. These people are always on the go, focused on moving straight ahead—they don't speak, don't smile. But once they get down to the Block Party, they slow way down. No one's in a hurry; although they have to line up and wait to buy their barbecue, there's no pushing or shoving. They start smiling at one another, making actual eye contact, engaging in conversation. They relax and enjoy the moment.

Here's my theory—and I've studied this out: For years, I kept bees in our backyard and there's an art to it. To harvest the honey without getting stung all over, you have to puff smoke into the hive to settle the bees. Well, that's exactly what we do to those New Yorkers in Madison Square Park—*we smoke 'em*. That aroma coming off the pits isn't just the smell of what's for dinner. It's a reminder: Take a moment, breathe a little deeper, worry a little less, and laugh a little more.

When people visit me at 17th Street, they come looking for some kind of barbecue messiah and instead find that I'm just like them, which is why they relate to me, I guess. These folks come to talk about barbecue and get some tips. But mostly they want to tell me how they do it, and they want to hear that they're doing it right. They also want to talk about their own barbecue experiences, or the way barbecue makes them feel. They walk into the restaurant, and they bring us their families, their memories, and their dreams.

I've come to realize that barbecue offers people salvation and a way of assembling their own congregations. I've seen barbecue revitalize towns and rehabilitate men. I've watched longtime legends finally get their due and young guns bring new spirit and creativity to the game. I've had thousands of visits from and conversations with people from all over the world who are drawn to the fire and smoke at 17th Street and who, having partaken of communion from our bar, are now part of our extended barbecue family.

And now here you are, giving it up to the gods of smoke and fire and meat.

Welcome to the fold.

 **Mike**

LONG BEFORE he opened 17th Street, my daddy loved feeding people. At every family party, the main event was his barbecue, and for the holidays he smoked hams and turkeys as gifts for all the relatives. For much of my childhood, he was in an altogether different line of work—owner and operator of the Murphysboro Dental Lab (which remains in business today and is one of the oldest commercial establishments in town)—but even then he cooked every day: vats of soup and stew and chili balanced precariously on Bunsen burners alongside pots of wax melting for denture molds. Various and sundry friends would show up for lunch, and the UPS man learned to time his deliveries accordingly.

WE WERE FOODIES BEFORE THE TERM WAS INVENTED. Not the kind of foodies who run around to fancy or trendy restaurants—we didn't have any of those in Murphysboro. Although eating our way through New Orleans was our idea of a family vacation, we knew that food simply didn't get any better than what we made at home. Our family would occasionally eat barbecue from local restaurants, but nothing was ever as good as the stuff from our own backyard. I learned at an early age that not all deviled eggs are created equal (the devil is, quite literally, in the details) and that the best ones were made by Aunt Jeanette and Aunt Joyce (page 62). Nobody made baked beans like Aunt Judy, or cornbread like Uncle John, and Mama Faye's barbecue sauce was legendary. At church suppers and community gatherings, we made a beeline for the platters we'd brought ourselves.

Big, boisterous family gatherings loom large in my memory—afternoons and evenings filled with lots of loud storytelling, strong opinions, and even stronger drinks. Everyone brought a specialty or two, and the table brimmed with slaws and salads, baked beans, collards, mac and cheese, fruit pies and cobblers. Daddy always manned the pit, and there was always a jug of Mama Faye's barbecue sauce—plus fresh bottles for everyone to take home.

When I flew the nest, went to journalism school, and moved to Texas, I explored trendy restaurants and food movements and sought out good barbecue all over the greater Dallas area. I came to appreciate Texas-style beef brisket and ribs, but it didn't take me home. Moving to Boston put me even farther away from my family's home cooking. I devised a way to cope with this deprivation. I brought an extra suitcase whenever I flew home for a visit, and I figured out how to pack it very efficiently: fifteen frozen racks of ribs, with one-pound packages of pulled pork tucked in around the edges, and a few half-chickens squeezed in for good measure, so it weighed in at about forty-nine pounds, just light enough to be under the FAA limit for checked baggage.

A POST-IT NOTE BROUGHT ME BACK TO MURPHYSBORO and into the family business. In 2000, newly divorced and yearning for home, I began spending more time there just as Daddy's growing fame on the barbecue circuit got to the point where the 17th Street office was flooded with PR requests. I'd spent the past dozen years working in advertising, and my dad would ask me for the occasional favor. One day he handed me a slip of paper and asked me to return a call. Turned out it was an editor at *Martha Stewart Living* who was writing about mail-order barbecue. But because it'd taken three weeks to get back to her, the piece had already been written. "Daddy! You missed a big opportunity," I said. "From now on, give all those little scraps of paper to me."

Barbecue drew me closer to my extended family and my daddy. I carted my son and daughter, Woody and Faye Landess (named after her barbecue-sauce-making great-grandmother), back and forth from the Boston area, and they did their own growing-up-barbecue in Murphysboro. They labeled and filled countless bottles with our special dry rub, endured summer stints in the restaurant, and slung barbecue at state fairs and at festivals around the country. They learned that the culture and teen life of Southern Illinois is vastly different from that of the seaside town in which they were raised. They now know how to drive a Ford 350, properly clean a pit, prep a rack of ribs, and make a mean barbecue sandwich.

Most important, they continue to learn from their Grampy Mike the lessons I learned long ago: "People are people." "You can't soar with the eagles if you're out hootin' with the owls all night." And, most definitely, "Life is too short for a half-rack."

 **Amy**

VERNACULAR

BARBECUE SPOKEN HERE

BARBECUE HAS its own language of smoke, spice, meat, and sauce—plus some actual lingo. Every region has its own dialect, and each barbecuer speaks in their very own accent. A Texan might offer you a freshly smoked hot gut (sausage), a North Carolinian might invite you to a pig pickin' (pig roast), and folks in our neck of the woods are likely to serve you a pork steak (cut from the butt end of a pork shoulder).

In our very own particular patois, we've been known to put it this way:

BARBECUE = FOOD + FAMILY + LOVE

When we serve up our barbecue, be it in our backyard or at our restaurant, in a festival tent, or right here in this book, we are bringing you into our family and our home. By way of a warm welcome, we want to take make sure you're not confused by any of our idiosyncratic turns of phrase or odd terminology.

First of all, we're church-going God-fearing and Christians, and we intend neither blasphemy nor disrespect with our language and our metaphors. We believe God has a sense of humor. Our spiritual leaders certainly do—our rector even sports a "Praise the Lard" T-shirt.

A tidbit of geography: We're tucked in at the southern tip of Illinois, 336 miles from Chicago. Our corner of the world is Southern Illinois—that's with a capital *S*. The nearest large airport is two hours away in St. Louis, Missouri, and we're only three hours from both Memphis and Nashville, in Tennessee. We are in close proximity to the point where the mighty Ohio and Mississippi Rivers meet—we're decidedly Midwestern with a strong Southern twang.

Some vocabulary: What we call a **peanut roll** isn't a roll at all, it's a cakey sort of thing and it's yummy. And there's a peculiar slaw–chow chow hybrid known to us simply as **chow**. For us, **bark** much less often refers to what you'd find on a tree than it does the delicious crust on a piece of barbecue, and **nose** is a term for the fatty part of a brisket (as is **point** or **deckle**). A few words we use interchangeably: **pit**, **smoker**, **cooker**, **grill**. A pit is *not* a hole in the ground, and a grill is generally a device on which we use direct, high heat. A **cook** is the process of cooking a piece of meat on the pit, not the person preparing it—that would be the **pit boss**, not to be confused with the **pitmaster**. This honorific is bestowed upon barbecuers of the highest order—you can't rightfully call yourself a pitmaster until, through time and trial, you have mastered the art of barbecue. Calling yourself a pitmaster without having earned the title just is not cool.

When it comes to recipe yields and portion sizes, we speak a language of abundance. Although many of our recipes are easy to scale down, others, not so much. In those cases—from pork shoulder to brisket dumplings, savory cheesecake to beer brats, vat of punch to pitcher of margaritas—there's plenty to go around, whether it's to fill the freezer, serve at a dinner party, take to a neighbor, or contribute to the potluck table at a contest or a church supper.

One last note: In the wider world, barbecue is a noun. It's meat, slow-smoked over aromatic wood, dusted with spices, and swizzled with sauce. Barbecue is also a verb, referring to the action of cooking barbecue. Certain self-appointed barbecue police (vigilantes, really) will chide you for using the term to refer to cooking hamburgers and hot dogs, which are usually grilled directly over high heat. We don't care what you call 'em. It's all good.

THE FIRM FOUNDATION

TRIED-AND-TRUE

PERSONAL PANTRY

PREFERENCES

F OR SOME of the recipes in this book, we're specific and particular about a few key ingredients. We're pretty frugal and we don't fuss about much, but there are certain brands and ingredients that make a real difference in food flavor, nuance, and dimension. These are areas where we don't skimp because the difference in quality is distinct. Bargain ingredients make sense only when they're a value; when you sacrifice flavor, it becomes waste. We also use local brands and ingredients to add local flavor and make things uniquely ours, and we encourage you to do the same.

Butter Real. Unsalted.

Cane syrup The complex flavor of cane syrup adds a special touch to cocktails and baked goods. Cane syrup is made from the juice that's squeezed from sugarcane stalks and boiled to evaporate the liquid and stabilize the sugars. The result is a rich syrup that's sweeter than molasses, with a deep caramel flavor. Once a standard for cooking, and especially baking, cane syrup was replaced by the less-expensive refined sugars and corn syrup that proliferated in the market as sugar-cane growers realized they could make more money selling their cane to refineries rather than producing the cane syrup themselves. Even today, Steen's, one of the most popular brands, sells their own crop and buys cane juice to make their famous syrup. We're partial to Lavington Farms from South Carolina, and Poirier's from Louisiana, as well as Steen's, all available via mail order (see page 325).

King Arthur and White Lily flour All flour is not created equal; there are varying amounts of protein in each and that protein, when combined with moisture, is what creates gluten. Gluten provides structure to baked goods. Baking good bread requires a flour high in protein; less-dense baked goods, such as cakes and pastries, benefit from a flour with less protein. King Arthur has the highest amount of protein of the name-brand flours available, and White Lily, milled from soft winter wheat, has the least. King Arthur flour is unbleached, lending foods a fuller flavor. If not available at a grocery store in your area, both varieties are available for purchase on Amazon.

Honey We kept honeybees for years, and we used the honey from those hives in our famous baked beans recipe. We no longer keep bees, but we do collect honey from our local farmers' market and roadside stands wherever we travel. The flavors are as distinct as the clover, buckwheat, apple blossoms, or whatever the bees are pollinating. Even honey harvested from the same hive will have a different taste and color depending on whether it's removed in the spring, summer, or fall. Local honey from small producers will always have a more pronounced flavor than mass-produced honey.

Ketchup We use Hunt's or Red Gold ketchup because they are made with pure cane sugar, not high-fructose corn syrup. This makes an especially discernable difference in the flavor of sauces.

Lard and tallow We save pork and beef fat and render our own lard and tallow (for more on lard and tallow, see page 42).

Local soda Coca-Cola and Pepsi soft drinks, or soda, as we say in Southern Illinois, are sweetened with high-fructose corn syrup instead of liquid cane sugar. The exception is Mexican Coke, bottled by Coca-Cola in Mexico using liquid cane sugar. It's a cult favorite and can be found in Texas and select places nationwide. There's a distinct flavor difference; cane sugar soda tastes sweeter and cleaner, with no chemical aftertaste. At 17th Street, we sell a line of cherry, grapefruit, lemon-lime, and blueberry sodas made by Excel Bottling Company in Breese, Illinois, and root beer, ginger beer, and cream soda from Fitz's Bottling

Company in St. Louis, Missouri. Big Muddy Brewing, a microbrewery located in Murphysboro, is making a delicious root beer, too. Cheerwine is the popular local choice in North Carolina; Cannonborough Beverage Company is South Carolina's local go-to, and in the Northeast, it's Boylan. Izze brand sodas are sweetened only with natural fruit and they're available nationwide. These refreshing fizzy drinks taste great with a pulled pork sandwich. We also use these sodas in barbecue sauces and glazes, to both add flavor and thin the sauce without watering it down.

Pepper One of our rubs calls for a specific mesh size (a unit of measurement) or grind of pepper that can't be purchased at the grocery store but is available online. Using the specified grind is important. If the grind is too large, you'll feel like you're eating gravel; if it's too fine for certain recipes, it'll become pasty. You can grind peppercorns in a spice mill or coffee grinder, or put them a skillet and then crush them with a heavy saucepan. Other recipes call for coarsely ground black pepper, and for that you can use a pepper mill or buy coarsely ground black pepper in the spice section of the grocery store. See page 321 for online suppliers. We also specify ground white pepper in a number of recipes. You can buy this in a bottle, already ground, or you can buy white peppercorns and grind them yourself. White pepper has less heat than black pepper, and is more earthy and complex.

Pickle juice Always save the juice from any jar of pickles, whether store-bought or homemade. This seasoned vinegar adds zip to deviled eggs, chili, and all sorts of recipes.

Salt Use kosher salt unless otherwise specified.

Spices We're very particular about our spices, as they're the foundation of flavor. There's a distinct difference in the quality and consistency of spices you buy in grocery and big-box stores. You never quite know how long those bottles and tins have been sitting on the shelves, and even if the turnover is high, the spices at discount stores are less expensive because they're not top quality and not always consistent in flavor. We buy our spices exclusively from Townsend Spice in Melbourne, Arkansas. At home, we keep fairly small amounts of spices, storing them in a cool, dark cabinet and replacing them at least once a year, or whenever the color fades or they don't smell fresh and pungent.

Sugar Read the label and make sure it says "pure cane sugar." Sugar that is very inexpensive may be beet sugar instead of pure cane sugar. It's not the same substance and there will be a difference in texture and flavor in the finished recipe. Cane sugar is a superior product.

THE HOLY TRINITY

SEASONING, SMOKE, AND SAUCE

G REAT BARBECUE is *built*, layer by flavorful layer, and this chapter is all about the foundation of that deliciously balanced structure: seasoning, smoke, and sauce. The formulations and philosophies we share with you here come from a lifetime of trial and error and form the cornerstone of our barbecue: award-winning, accolade-garnering, and, most important, beloved by our guests and family—and that's the ultimate prize.

RUBS | SAUCES

RUBS			SAUCES
Pure Magic	29	36	Apple City Barbecue Sauce
Texas Forever Brisket Rub	30	37	Blackberry-Habanero Sauce
Java Jolt	31	38	Raspberry-Chipotle Sauce
Mustard Slather	31	39	Private Reserve Mustard Sauce
Sweet Chili Dry Rub	32	40	Hog Wash Vinegar Splash
Steakhouse Shake	32	41	Cheerwine Glaze
Basic Dry Rub	33	41	Apricot Glaze
Sweet Heat Dry Rub	33		

SMOKE STARTS WITH WOOD

Wood is one of the regional markers of barbecue, and each type imparts a specific flavor. That's why we call it an ingredient. You could cook meat with the exact same seasoning and sauce using different woods and come up with very different results. Wood is purely a matter of preference and availability. With the burgeoning popularity of barbecue, you can get almost any kind of wood shipped right to your door. But just because it's available, doesn't mean it's good. We're not huge fans of mesquite, for example, since we find it overpowering and harsh. We're fortunate to be able to source hickory, pecan, oak, apple, wild cherry, and peach within a five-mile radius of 17th Street. While it's fun to experiment, the wood that we have the easiest access to will always be our first choice.

We're partial to fruit woods, primarily because we're surrounded by apple, peach, and wild cherry trees. Beginning in the 1980s, we used the apple wood discarded by local orchards when they were pruning each spring. Now, having created huge demand for this wood, we have to pay for it.

Light Woods

Fruit woods are often described as having a mild, sweet smoke. Some people talk about flavors of wood like wine—nutty, jammy, vanilla—but we don't get any of that. We would never talk about a piece of pork tasting like a cherry lollipop, but wild cherry, in particular, does give meat a rich mahogany appearance. Pecan falls in the light-wood category and has a distinctive flavor that's stronger than apple or cherry.

Hard Woods

Hard woods have a stronger, more pronounced smoke. They're longer burning and well suited to bulk meats—shoulders, butts, briskets, and whole animals. That said, we use apple wood to smoke everything from baby back ribs and chicken to brisket and whole hogs. Really, it's just a matter of personal preference.

Hickory, one of the most popular woods used in barbecue, has the heartiest, most pungent smoke. Be careful. It's easy to overdo it with hickory.

Oak produces a heavy, clean smoke, and it's a slow-burning wood perfect for longer cooks. There are a number of varieties of oak. Post oak is synonymous with Texas barbecue. White and red oak are burned in many legendary barbecue places in the Carolinas.

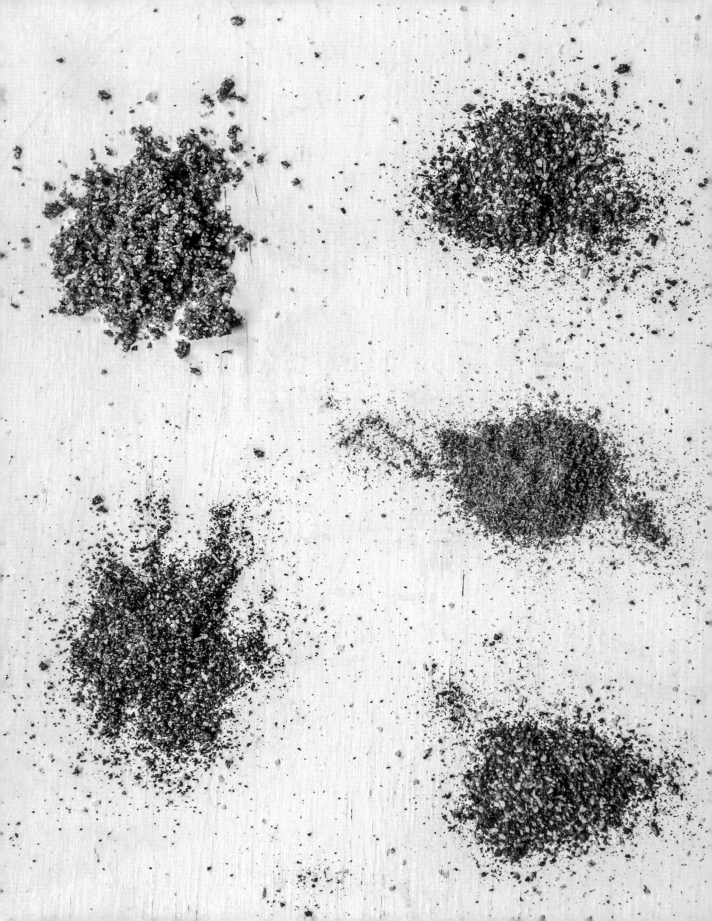

Rubs

While the flavor profile of our restaurant barbecue is savory and traditional, at home and in our catering operation we like to experiment with all sorts of flavors and ingredients. Dry rubs are applied to meat before smoking, and they help form the delicious, flavorful "bark" on the outside of the meat. You can also use them to enhance the flavor of many other foods.

PURE MAGIC

MAKES ABOUT 2¼ CUPS

For our favorite rub, the spices are ground to a fine powder; you'll need a spice mill or coffee grinder. Spice particles that are all the same size create a rub that melts when used on meat. No one flavor will predominate, and you won't feel gritty spice particles when you're eating. The combination of spices is savory, with just a little sweetness. Use leftover rub as called for in a variety of recipes in this book. You'll also find yourself reaching for this well-balanced all-purpose rub for all kinds of meat, as well as fish, vegetables, french fries, and popcorn.

½ cup sweet Hungarian paprika

¼ cup kosher salt

¼ cup sugar

¼ cup granulated garlic

¼ cup chili powder

¼ cup ground cumin

1 tablespoon dry mustard

1 tablespoon coarsely ground black pepper

1 teaspoon cayenne pepper

Mix all the ingredients. Using a spice mill or coffee grinder, blend ¼ cup at a time to a powder-like consistency so that all of the spice particles are relatively the same size.

Store in a tightly covered container in a cool, dark place. The rub keeps for about 6 months, or until the color or pungent aroma fades.

Variation: To make this rub a little spicier, increase the mustard and black pepper to 2 tablespoons each.

TEXAS FOREVER BRISKET RUB

MAKES ABOUT 2 CUPS

We add a little granulated garlic to our version of the classic Texas brisket rub. Using 18-mesh coarse ground black pepper is important in this recipe: The size of the grind in rubs affects the flavor as it hits your tongue, and too fine a grind will turn the rub into a paste-like consistency. We've provided a source for 18-mesh coarse ground black pepper in the Resources section (see page 321). Alternatively, you can use a spice mill or coffee grinder to coarsely grind whole peppercorns or you can put whole black peppercorns in a skillet and then use a smaller saucepan to press down on top of them with a lot of pressure to crush and grind them. Brisket and beef ribs are high in fat, and the fat renders during the smoking process and combines with the coarse pepper to create a thick bark that helps seal in moisture and add texture and flavor to the meat.

1½ cups 18-mesh ground black pepper or coarsely ground black pepper

¼ cup kosher salt

3 tablespoons granulated garlic

Combine all the ingredients in a small bowl and mix with a whisk to blend evenly. Store in a tightly covered container in a cool, dark place. The rub keeps for about 6 months, or until the color or pungent aroma fades.

JAVA JOLT

MAKES ABOUT 1 CUP

Cocoa and coffee are the surprise ingredients in this complex rub that pairs well with beef.

6 tablespoons ground espresso beans

2 tablespoons unsweetened cocoa

2 tablespoons coarsely ground black pepper

4 teaspoons sugar

4 teaspoons kosher salt

Combine all the ingredients in a small bowl and mix with a whisk to blend evenly. Store in a tightly covered container in a cool, dark place. The rub keeps for about 6 months, or until the color or pungent aroma fades.

MUSTARD SLATHER

MAKES 2 CUPS

Use this on brisket, pork shoulder or butt, and beef or pork loin to protect the surface and help the rub adhere to the meat. Use a 50/50 ratio of mustard and pickle juice to make the amount you think you'll need. Save and sterilize a plastic condiment bottle to use for storing and applying the slather.

1 cup prepared yellow mustard (we use French's)
1 cup pickle juice

Stir together in a large bowl. Decant into a squeeze bottle or glass jar. Store in the refrigerator; keeps indefinitely. To use, squirt or pour a generous portion over the meat and smear it around with your hand to lightly coat.

SWEET CHILI DRY RUB

MAKES ABOUT 2 CUPS

A blend of savory and sweet, with a bit of heat on the back end, this rub is delicious on pork and poultry.

¾ cups packed dark brown sugar

¼ cup turbinado sugar (such as Sugar in the Raw)

¼ cup kosher salt

¼ cup granulated sugar

3 tablespoons chili powder

2 tablespoons dry mustard

2 tablespoons granulated garlic

2 tablespoons granulated onion

2 tablespoons sweet Hungarian paprika

1 teaspoon cayenne pepper

Combine all the ingredients in a small bowl and mix with a whisk to blend evenly. Store in a tightly covered container in a cool, dark place. The rub keeps for about 6 months, or until the color or pungent aroma fades.

STEAKHOUSE SHAKE

MAKES ABOUT ½ CUP

This savory blend tastes great on hamburgers, steaks, brisket, and beef ribs.

2 tablespoons dry mustard

2 tablespoons granulated garlic

2 teaspoons coarsely ground black pepper

1½ teaspoons kosher salt

1 teaspoon smoked sweet Spanish paprika

½ teaspoon dried thyme

½ teaspoon cayenne pepper

Combine all the ingredients in a small bowl and mix with a whisk to blend evenly. Store in a tightly covered container in a cool, dark place. Keeps for about 6 months, or until the color or pungent aroma fades.

BASIC DRY RUB

MAKES ABOUT ½ CUP

The coarse grinds of the turbinado sugar and black pepper create extra texture for this classic dry rub with a hint of sweet heat.

2 tablespoons sweet Hungarian paprika

1 tablespoon turbinado sugar (such as Sugar in the Raw)

1 tablespoon dark brown sugar

1 tablespoon ground chipotle

1½ teaspoons coarsely ground black pepper

1½ teaspoons cayenne pepper

1½ teaspoons ground cumin

1½ teaspoons granulated onion

1½ teaspoons granulated garlic

Combine all the ingredients in a small bowl and mix with a whisk to blend evenly. Store in a tightly covered container in a cool, dark place. The rub keeps for about 6 months, or until the color or pungent aroma fades.

SWEET HEAT DRY RUB

MAKES ABOUT 1 CUP

A combination of sugars and molasses, along with chile powder and cayenne, lends sweetness and heat to this hot, sticky, spicy rub.

6 tablespoons dark brown sugar

1 tablespoon coarsely ground black pepper

1 tablespoon turbinado sugar (such as Sugar in the Raw)

1½ teaspoons molasses powder (see Resources, page 321)

1½ teaspoons kosher salt

½ teaspoon ground chipotle

¼ teaspoon smoked sweet Spanish paprika

¼ teaspoon cayenne pepper

Combine all the ingredients in a small bowl and mix with a whisk to blend evenly. Store in a tightly covered container in a cool, dark place. The rub keeps for about 6 months, or until the color or pungent aroma fades.

Sauces

At barbecue shrines across the country, you'll find just one or maybe two sauces on the table. At 17th Street, for years, we had only our original sauce and a spicier version called A Little Kick.

Then we began seeing the "six-pack," six squeeze bottles of sauce on a table, perhaps in repurposed cardboard beer cartons. To us, that felt homogenized, and as though the restaurant owner didn't have a specific point of view. We'd see people testing each one and shaking their heads. There were too many choices and maybe not enough good ones.

But we've changed our opinion. People like variety and they've come to expect it. We've created a few new sauces for specific menu items, and locals know to ask for a bottle to be brought to the table. We developed each sauce carefully and we're proud to put our name on them. If you're going to put out multiple bottles, make sure each one has earned its space on the table.

Sweet, savory, fruity, tangy, hot—flavor profiles run the gamut. Most people's favorite is usually influenced by a childhood taste memory. This is an area where it's fun to play. Our one adamant rule is that the smoke flavor should come from the cooker, not a bottle. In other words, liquid smoke is the devil. It adheres to the roof of the mouth and hangs there for hours, ruining the effort and hard work you put into a piece of meat. If you use a bottled sauce as a base to create a new sauce, be sure to read the ingredients listed on the label and choose one without liquid smoke.

PROPER USE OF BARBECUE SAUCE

A common mistake in barbecue is adding sauce too early in the cooking process. Most barbecue sauce contains sugar, and adding it too early will cause the surface of the meat to char. If you're adding sauce to ribs or chicken cooked over indirect heat, brush it on lightly about 20 minutes before you take it off the cooker. If you're grilling over direct heat, add the sauce just a few minutes before you pull the meat off the cooker.

We prefer thin sauce, brushed on in one or two light coats that seep into the meat to build up flavor, instead of using thick sauce that sits on top of the meat. Heat the sauce to between 120° and 140° before brushing for best results.

APPLE CITY BARBECUE SAUCE

MAKES ABOUT 2 CUPS

This is the sauce that has won us dozens of awards and accolades on the competition circuit. It's a harmonious combination of ketchup, vinegar, and mustard—the three ingredients that typically set regional barbecue styles apart from one another—along with fresh grated apple, a nod to the apple orchards surrounding Murphysboro. This sauce is a favorite on ribs and pulled pork sandwiches, as well as on chicken and hamburgers.

¾ cup ketchup (made with cane sugar, such as Red Gold or Hunt's)

⅔ cup rice vinegar

1½ cups apple cider

¼ cup apple cider vinegar

¼ cup packed light brown sugar

¼ cup Worcestershire sauce

2 teaspoons prepared yellow mustard

½ teaspoon granulated garlic

⅛ teaspoon ground white pepper

⅛ teaspoon cayenne pepper

⅓ cup bacon bits (real, not imitation), ground in a spice mill

⅓ cup grated peeled apple

⅓ cup grated onion

2 teaspoons grated green pepper

Combine the ketchup, rice vinegar, apple juice, cider vinegar, brown sugar, Worcestershire sauce, mustard, granulated garlic, white pepper, cayenne, and bacon bits in a large saucepan. Bring to a boil, stir in the apple, onion, and green pepper, then lower the heat. Simmer the sauce, stirring often, for 10 to 15 minutes, until it thickens slightly. Decant into a mason jar, cover, and refrigerate; the sauce will keep for at least a month. Warm or bring to room temperature before serving.

Variation: To make this sauce a little hotter, add more cayenne pepper to taste, another ¼ to ½ teaspoon. Be careful; a little goes a long way.

BLACKBERRY-HABANERO SAUCE

MAKES ABOUT 4 CUPS

Adding habanero peppers and sriracha to a fresh blackberry base balances the sweetness of the fruit. Have no fear, the hot sauce and habanero bring just a nice little bite, not a blast of heat. This is best made at the height of blackberry season, which is all too brief. We use this sauce on all types of poultry and pork; it's especially good on pork chops.

½ cup rice vinegar

3 tablespoons apple cider vinegar

3 tablespoons Worcestershire sauce

2 teaspoons Pure Magic dry rub (page 29) or your choice

1 quart blackberries

2 tablespoons tomato paste

2 tablespoons molasses

2 tablespoons pure cane syrup (see Resources, page 321)

2 teaspoons local honey

1 tablespoon light brown sugar

1 tablespoon blackberry preserves

¼ teaspoon minced seeded habanero pepper

⅛ teaspoon sriracha sauce

Combine the vinegars, Worcestershire sauce, dry rub, and blackberries in a medium saucepan. Bring to a boil, whisking constantly. Take the pan off the heat. Add the remaining ingredients and whisk until well combined. Decant into a mason jar and let cool. Cover and store in the refrigerator; the sauce will keep for at least 2 weeks. Warm or bring to room temperature before serving.

RASPBERRY-CHIPOTLE SAUCE

MAKES 2½ CUPS

Pepper gives plenty of punch to this fruity and complex sauce. It's excellent with poultry or pork. We often serve it with pork loin. Substitute cooked fresh cherries and cherry preserves during cherry season.

½ cup sugar

½ teaspoon granulated garlic

½ teaspoon ground chipotle

½ teaspoon red pepper flakes

½ teaspoon coarsely ground black pepper

1 pint raspberries

¾ cup ketchup (made with cane sugar, such as Red Gold or Hunt's)

½ cup raspberry preserves

¼ cup raspberry balsamic vinegar

¼ cup light corn syrup

2 tablespoons rice vinegar

1 tablespoon fresh lime juice

1 tablespoon bourbon (we use Maker's Mark)

1 teaspoon Worcestershire sauce

¼ teaspoon hot sauce (we use Texas Pete)

½ jalapeño pepper, seeded

Whisk together the sugar, garlic, chipotle, pepper flakes, and black pepper in a small bowl. In a large saucepan, whisk together all the remaining ingredients except the jalapeño pepper. Whisk in the spice mixture and bring to a boil, then lower the heat and simmer, stirring often, for 10 minutes. Add the jalapeño and continue to simmer, stirring frequently, for 15 to 20 minutes, until the sauce thickens to a jammy, but still pourable, consistency. Discard the jalapeño. Decant the sauce into a mason jar; cool, cover, and store in the refrigerator, where it will keep for at least 1 month. Warm or bring to room temperature before serving.

PRIVATE RESERVE MUSTARD SAUCE

MAKES ABOUT 2½ CUPS

Our family has made this sharp, spicy mustard sauce for over eighty years, and we always have a batch on hand. Good on pork, poultry, hamburgers, and hot dogs, it's also wonderful drizzled on a chopped brisket or pastrami sandwiches.

1½ cups prepared yellow mustard (we use French's)

½ cup tomato paste

7 tablespoons light brown sugar

5 tablespoons apple cider vinegar

1 tablespoon Worcestershire sauce

½ teaspoon cayenne pepper

½ teaspoon ground black pepper

½ teaspoon granulated garlic

Whisk all the ingredients together in a small saucepan over medium heat. Simmer just until the sugar is dissolved. Decant into a mason jar; cool, cover, and store in the refrigerator, where the sauce will keep for 2 months. Bring to room temperature before serving.

HOG WASH VINEGAR SPLASH

MAKES ABOUT 10 CUPS

A staple in North Carolina, this bright, acidic sauce is splashed liberally over a whole hog or pork butt or shoulder. The vinegar helps cleanse your palate and counteracts the rich fat in the meat. It's also surprisingly good on brisket. We use the sauce on the meat as we're pulling it, and we add another standard barbecue sauce when we're making a sandwich. If you're cooking a whole hog, you'll use the better part of the quantity here. If you're cooking a pork butt, shoulder, or brisket, you'll use much less. You can easily halve the recipe, but you might as well make the whole thing as it's primarily vinegar and keeps indefinitely. Five percent acidity is typical for cider vinegar, and it's essential for this recipe so check the label.

1½ cups sugar

½ gallon apple cider vinegar, 5 percent acidity

1 cup ketchup (made with cane sugar, such as Red Gold or Hunt's)

½ cup Worcestershire sauce

2 tablespoons red pepper flakes

3¾ teaspoons chili powder

1 tablespoon ground cumin

2¼ teaspoons granulated garlic

2¼ teaspoons granulated onion

1½ teaspoons cayenne pepper

Combine the sugar, vinegar, ketchup, and Worcestershire sauce in a large stockpot over high heat and heat just until steaming. While the liquid is warming, whisk together the red pepper flakes, chili powder, cumin, granulated garlic, granulated onion, and cayenne in a small bowl. Take the pan off the heat and stir in the spice mixture. Cool to room temperature. Using a funnel, decant ½ gallon of the sauce back into the vinegar jug, frequently pausing to stir to keep the spices well distributed as you're pouring. Funnel the excess 2 cups into plastic squeeze bottles or a mason jar. Keeps indefinitely. Shake well before using.

CHEERWINE GLAZE

MAKES ABOUT 1½ CUPS

Sweet and bursting with cherry flavor, this glaze is delicious drizzled over cooker-smoked ham or pork loin.

1 cup Cheerwine or other local cherry soda made with cane syrup

10 fresh sour cherries, pitted and diced, or ¼ cup chopped dried cherries

½ cup packed light brown sugar

1 cup cherry preserves

2 tablespoons rice vinegar

1 teaspoon fresh lemon juice

½ teaspoon Frank's RedHot sauce

¼ teaspoon finely grated lemon zest

⅛ teaspoon red pepper flakes

Combine all the ingredients in a medium saucepan and bring to a simmer. Reduce the heat and continue simmering gently, stirring constantly, for about 10 minutes, until slightly syrupy. Use immediately or decant into a mason jar. The glaze will keep, refrigerated, for about 2 weeks. Best used warm.

APRICOT GLAZE

MAKES ABOUT 1½ CUPS

The fresh and bright flavors of apricot and lime are spiked with a little heat. The sauce pairs well with pork loin, pork chops, or ribs if you like a sweeter flavor profile.

One 12-ounce bottle ginger beer

1 cup apricot preserves

2 tablespoons maple syrup

1 fresh apricot, diced, or 6 dried apricots, chopped

1 tablespoon minced candied ginger

1½ teaspoons Dijon mustard

1½ teaspoons Frank's RedHot sauce

¼ teaspoon finely grated lime zest

1 teaspoon fresh lime juice

¼ teaspoon red pepper flakes

Follow the method for Cheerwine Glaze (above).

IN PRAISE OF LARD AND TALLOW

As more and more evidence points to the unhealthy qualities of canola and vegetable oils, pure animal fats are now back in fashion. Mike, of course, gets a huge kick out of this.

Hog Fat

Lard Packaged rendered lard is available on supermarket shelves, but be sure to read the label, since it's likely hydrogenated and contains preservatives and chemicals. Lard purchased from a farmers' market or a local butcher is a better choice. Or, better yet, render it yourself (see below).

Leaf lard is the pure fat from around the pig's kidneys. This is the cleanest fat on the animal. In order to have a pure white, odorless leaf lard to use for baking, rendering it properly is critical.

Fatback is the layer of fat directly below the skin, along the back of the hog on its shoulder and rump. You can buy it in pieces, often with the skin still attached. Rendered fatback is excellent for frying or sautéing.

Beef Tallow

Excellent for frying, beef tallow is the rendered form of the nutrient-rich fat around the cow's organs, particularly from the kidney region. This natural fat contains 55 percent saturated fats and 40 percent monounsaturated fats, which are both heat stable, and its 400° to 420° smoke point makes it excellent for frying.

Rendering Lard and Tallow

Start with at least 2 pounds of fat, enough to make the whole process worth your while. We process quite a bit of lard so we use a grinder, but if you don't have a grinder you can simply cut the lard into 1- to 2-inch pieces. Put the ground or chopped fat in a saucepan over lowest heat. (Alternatively, put it in a heavy-bottom pot, cover, and set in a 200° oven.) As the fat melts, any pieces of meat or tissue will separate out and settle on the bottom of the pan. Occasionally remove them with a skimmer; if left in too long, those pieces of meat will begin to cook and burn, giving the fat an overly meaty smell and taste (this is especially crucial with leaf lard, which should have no porky aroma whatsoever). Reserve the meaty bits.

While the fat is melting, layer a piece of cheesecloth inside a colander and set it over a large heatproof bowl or another saucepan.

Depending upon how much fat you are working with, it will take at least an hour to render. Once all of the fat is visibly melted, carefully ladle or pour it through the cheesecloth-lined colander. Ladle the strained lard or tallow into mason jars (we like to use the 4-ounce jelly size for pre-portioned amounts of leaf lard for baking). Let it cool and solidify, then cover and store in the refrigerator indefinitely. Use leaf lard for baking and regular lard and tallow for frying.

You can return the bits of skimmed meat to the saucepan and fry them until crispy and brown. These cracklin's can be used to garnish salads or baked potatoes, or as toppings on macaroni and cheese or other side dishes.

FAMILY HEIRLOOM

Mike's daddy, Leon Mills, made barbecue for the family and for the neighborhood at large. That sweet smoky aroma from the pit having its effect, various folks would bring their own meat over and he'd smoke it for them. Once they'd tasted Mama Faye's barbecue sauce, they wanted some of that, too. Family and friends saved and sterilized glass ketchup bottles and food jars so they could bring them back for refills.

When Mama Faye was widowed with three little children still at home, she began selling the sauce as a sideline so she could make a little extra money. Decades later, when I was growing up, she was still in the business, and a bottle of that sauce was a fixture on our family table—an essential condiment for ribs, burgers, sandwiches, and holiday feasts of pit-smoked ham and turkey.

From the time I was very young, I spent Saturday nights at Mama Faye's. Her house smelled of Estée Lauder Youth Dew intermingled with the sweet, sharp vinegar-and-brown-sugar aroma that emanated from the pot of sauce perpetually simmering on the stove. We had a routine: Mama Faye fixed me a pear salad—a canned pear, a dollop of mayonnaise in the hollow, and a sprinkling of shredded cheddar cheese, all atop a lettuce leaf and served on a lettuce ware plate she made in one of her ceramics classes. She painted my nails while we watched Lawrence Welk, and before bed she wrapped my long hair in sponge rollers so it would be wavy for church the next morning.

The recipe remained a closely guarded secret that Mama Faye shared only with her children—and not with their spouses. For the first ten years that we owned 17th Street, though she was well into her eighties, Mama Faye and only Mama Faye made the gallons of sauce for the restaurant every week. All told, she made that barbecue sauce in quantity every week for more than sixty years.

When 17th Street really took off, however, Daddy had to invest in a thirty-gallon sauce pot, and the production became too much for Mama Faye. Then it was Daddy who cooked up vat after vat himself. As miffed as she was that he tinkered just a bit with her original recipe, she was pretty proud when his Apple City Barbecue Sauce (page 36) swept the competition circuit. No doubt she would be amazed that we now ship our sauce all over the world.

=Amy=

SAYING GRACE

APPETIZERS AND OTHER OPENERS

We're checking all the boxes—sweet, smoky, spicy, creamy, and, of course, fried. These tantalizing starters pave the way for any party or meal where barbecue is the main event. Wings are both smoked and grilled, bacon is lacquered with sweet heat, and we've reimagined favorite Asian appetizers in a barbecue-centric way, cleverly incorporating leftover barbecue meat and sides. Vidalia onions star in a show-stoppingly savory, creamy dip. Simple from-scratch dressings and sauces make classic starters sing. Here and there, some assembly is required, but the reward is extras to fill your freezer. Choirs of angels have been heard by folks digging into these tasty apps. Here's hoping our standby favorites make their way into your party rotation.

PICKLED RED ONIONS

MAKES 2 PINTS

Vibrant pickled red onions are traditionally served with brisket and beef ribs at many barbecue institutions. We keep a jar in our refrigerator at home, since they're great as an addition to any sandwich or relish tray, or as a quick snack right out of the jar.

2 large red onions, sliced into ¼-inch-thick rings

1 cup apple cider vinegar or rice vinegar

1 teaspoon sugar

1 teaspoon kosher salt

10 pink or black peppercorns

10 allspice berries

4 to 6 sprigs thyme (optional)

2 small dried chile peppers (optional)

Fill a medium saucepan with water and bring to a boil. Add the onions and boil for 1 minute. Take the pan off the heat and drain. Return the onions to the pan and stir in the vinegar, sugar, and salt. Add just enough water to bring the liquid level to the top of the onions. Bring to a boil, then lower the heat and simmer for 1 minute.

Divide the peppercorns and allspice berries between two pint glass jars. If desired, add a few sprigs thyme and a chile pepper to each jar. Divide the onions between the jars and pour in the hot vinegar mixture to cover. Stir gently to distribute the seasonings. Cover tightly and let cool. Store in the refrigerator for up to 2 weeks.

LACQUERED BACON

**MAKES 10 TO 22 STRIPS BACON,
DEPENDING ON THE BRAND AND
HOW THICK IT'S CUT**

These sweet, sticky candied bacon strips disappear quickly. We defy you or your family members not to eat a single strip as you pass through the kitchen and eye them cooling on a wire rack. They're a special treat with eggs or crumbled on top of a breakfast casserole, and perfect as an addition to the Magic Mary bar (see page 276). We often break them into pieces and sprinkle on top of pancakes, cupcakes, and brownies. Dip one end into melted chocolate for a sinful treat.

1 cup packed light brown sugar	1 teaspoon cayenne pepper	1 pound bacon (thick-cut works best)

Preheat the oven to 400°, with two racks centered. Line two rimmed baking sheets with aluminum foil and top with wire racks.

Thoroughly mix the brown sugar and cayenne in a small bowl. Spread the mixture on a plate. Press one side of each piece of bacon into the mixture.

Arrange the bacon, sugared side up, on the racks. Bake for 20 to 25 minutes, rotating the pans midway through the baking, until the fat has rendered out of the bacon and the bacon is mahogany in color and beautifully caramelized. Allow to cool completely before serving.

PIQUANT PIMENTO CHEESE

MAKES ABOUT 2 CUPS

Although pimento cheese was invented in the North, it's now considered a Southern food group, with dozens of variations on the recipe. For her version, Mama Faye grated a large block of Velveeta cheese, which made it extra creamy and perfect for slathering on celery for school lunches or party appetizers, or spreading on spongy white Bunny Bread.

Today we use sharp cheddar instead of Velveeta, but grating remains one of the secrets. Don't skimp on the work—never buy packaged grated cheese, which contains additives that throw off the consistency of the spread. At 17th Street, we add a bit of wing sauce for a special zing. We serve it with thick slices of our all-beef sausage and classic crackers as an appetizer, slather it on burgers (page 138), or serve up a big bowl with a variety of crackers and celery sticks for parties. This recipe is best made a day or two ahead so all the flavors can meld.

2 whole canned pimentos, very thoroughly drained

½ pound sharp cheddar cheese, grated (2 cups)

2 to 3 scallions, finely chopped (¼ cup)

2 tablespoons sugar

1 teaspoon Worcestershire sauce

1 teaspoon 17th Street Wing Sauce (page 56) or your favorite hot sauce

½ cup mayonnaise (we use Hellmann's)

Slice the pimentos open to lay flat and set them out on a double layer of paper towels, blotting the tops with more towels to remove as much moisture as possible. Chop coarsely.

Evenly spread one-third of the cheese in the bowl of a food processor. Layer in the pimentos, scallions, sugar, Worcestershire sauce, wing sauce, and mayonnaise, followed by another third of the cheese. Use 20 to 25 very brief pulses to process just enough to uniformly blend—the mixture should be very chunky. Alternatively, mix all of the ingredients together by hand. Scrape into a bowl and fold in the remaining cheese. Transfer to a serving bowl, cover, and chill several hours or overnight before serving. Refrigerated and covered, the cheese keeps 1 week.

AIN'T NO THANG BUT A CHICKEN WING

MAKES ABOUT 16 WHOLE WINGS OR ABOUT 36 FLATS AND DRUMETTES

Our version of chicken wings tops several "best wings" lists, including one compiled by *Food & Wine* magazine. The secret is twofold: a two-step cooking method and our spicy wing sauce. Our wings are first smoked, then finished on the grill to crisp the skin before being mopped with the sauce. The combination of smoke and char and spice is unbeatable.

2 pounds chicken wings, whole or split into flats and drumettes, tips removed

Garlic salt

Pure Magic dry rub (page 29) or your choice

17th Street Wing Sauce (page 56), warm

Blue Cheese Dressing (page 57) or Buttermilk Ranch (page 57), for serving

Celery and carrot sticks, for serving

2 pounds good-quality lump charcoal (we use Royal Oak)

1 small (8-inch) piece of apple wood or 2 store-bought chunks

Prep the wings: Very lightly season the wings with garlic salt, coating them so thinly that it's barely visible. Set the wings on a baking sheet, cover with plastic wrap, and refrigerate until you're ready to put them on the cooker.

Set up the cooker for indirect-heat smoking: Open the top and bottom vents. Pile 1 pound of the charcoal in one half of the cooker, leaving the other half empty. Load a charcoal chimney one-quarter full of charcoal and light it. When the coals in the chimney are glowing, dump them on the charcoal in the cooker. Set the wood on top of the coals, replace the grate, and put the wings over the side with no coals (the indirect cooking area).

Don't open the cooker for 30 minutes, but keep a close eye on the temperature (see page 84 for how best to assess and monitor cooker temperature); when it reaches 200°, which might happen very quickly, close the vents about halfway so that less air comes in to feed the fire and the heat in the cooker rises slowly. Let the temperature climb to between 225° and 250° (see page 77 for how to determine your target temperature).

After 30 minutes, open the lid and check the edges of the wings closest to the fire. If they look like they're beginning to brown, rotate the wings without flipping

them over, moving the pieces that are farthest away and placing them closest to the fire, and vice versa.

Close the lid and continue smoking the wings for another hour, checking the color and the edges every 20 minutes. Never flip the pieces over; just continue rotating them to cook evenly. If at any point the temperature climbs above your target by more than 5°, close the top and bottom vents further so that even less air comes in to feed the fire.

After the wings have been on the cooker for 1½ hours, reload the chimney halfway with charcoal and light it; you'll need additional hot coals to sear the wings at the finishing stage, after they're done smoking. Use an instant-read thermometer to check for doneness: Insert the probe into the thickest part of a wing. When the wings reach 155°, pull them off the cooker and set them aside on a baking sheet. (At this point the wings can be cooled, packed into freezer bags, and refrigerated for up to 5 days or frozen for up to 3 months.)

Add the chimneyful of hot coals to the cooker, spreading them out all over the bottom for direct cooking. Replace the grate. Put the wings back on the cooker and sprinkle with dry rub. Sear for 2 to 4 minutes on each side, flipping once, just until charred but not burned, and the internal temperature is 165°.

Sprinkle the wings with a final light coat of dry rub and mop them with wing sauce. Pull the wings off the cooker and serve immediately with dressing and celery and carrot sticks.

17th Street Wing Sauce

MAKES ABOUT 2½ CUPS

We always have a jar of this wing sauce in our refrigerator. Not only does it add just the right amount of smooth heat to wings, it can also be substituted for hot sauce in many recipes. We use it in our deviled eggs (page 62) as well. Brush it on grilled chicken to top a fresh green salad or on a hamburger for an extra spicy kick.

2 cups Frank's RedHot sauce

1 teaspoon granulated garlic

¼ teaspoon chili powder

8 tablespoons (1 stick) cold unsalted butter, cut into several pieces

Combine all the ingredients except the butter in a medium saucepan. Cook over medium heat, whisking constantly to prevent scorching. As soon as the mixture begins to simmer, take the pan from the heat and drop in the butter pieces, stirring until melted and incorporated.

Use immediately or decant into a mason jar, cover, and store in the refrigerator; the sauce keeps for at least 1 month. Warm before using.

Blue Cheese Dressing

MAKES ABOUT 3 CUPS

A cool counterpoint to the heat of the wing sauce, this rich and creamy dressing is dotted with pungent bits of blue cheese. Use any leftover dressing as a dip for potato chips or vegetables, or to dress a wedge salad.

1 cup sour cream

1 cup mayonnaise (we use Hellmann's)

3 tablespoons red wine vinegar

1 teaspoon chopped garlic

½ teaspoon Worcestershire sauce

½ cup crumbled Roquefort

½ cup chopped fresh flat-leaf parsley

Kosher salt and freshly ground black pepper

Whisk together the sour cream, mayonnaise, vinegar, garlic, and Worcestershire sauce in a bowl. Using a rubber spatula, fold in the Roquefort and parsley until well incorporated. Season to taste with salt and pepper. Store in the refrigerator; the dressing will keep for at least 1 week.

Buttermilk Ranch

MAKES ABOUT 2 CUPS

The variety of fresh herbs used in our rendition of creamy ranch dressing gives it fresh, bright flavor. Use any leftover dressing as a dip for vegetables. We also put it in our Home-Style Potato Salad (page 211).

¾ cup full-fat buttermilk

½ cup sour cream

½ cup mayonnaise (we use Hellmann's)

2 tablespoons finely chopped scallions

2 tablespoons finely chopped fresh flat-leaf parsley

2 tablespoons chopped fresh chives

1 small garlic clove, minced

¼ teaspoon kosher salt

¼ teaspoon coarsely ground black pepper

Whisk together all the ingredients in a medium bowl. Decant into a mason jar, cover, and refrigerate; the dressing will keep for at least 1 week.

SOUL ROLLS

MAKES 24 ROLLS

We were introduced to Soul Rolls when we went to Washington, D.C., to participate in the Smithsonian Institution's celebration of American food on the Fourth of July. The plan was for us to give a talk and a barbecue demonstration right on the National Mall. Since we were making only a small amount of food (by our standards), we put a line out to some local folks about whether we might borrow equipment. Right away, we heard back from Mark Arnold, the chef at Old Glory Bar-B-Cue in Georgetown. Not only did he offer to drive his cooker down to the Mall at 5:00 a.m. on a national holiday, but he also made sure to include gloves, tongs, aluminum foil, and other items we might need. At the end of the day he took us to his restaurant for dinner. When a version of this appetizer showed up with a round of cocktails, we knew we'd found a man who understood the power of hospitality.

Soul Rolls are the barbecue version of a fried egg roll, and they get their name from the soul food—namely collards and barbecue—from which they're made. This is a genius way to use leftover meat and side dishes after a big barbecue feast or party. Start getting in the habit of freezing any leftover barbecue meat and scraps. While we've given specific ingredient amounts in the recipe, you can certainly vary this based on what you have on hand. Sometimes we might only use slaw; other times just collards. The one thing we wouldn't increase, though, is the corn. If you have too many kernels, they'll break through the egg roll wrappers.

There are about 24 wrappers per package. Once you get in the rhythm of filling and rolling, it's easy to make them all up and freeze what you don't use immediately. Or, if you want to make enough for a party, simply double or triple the amounts.

1 cup Brisket-Seasoned Collards (page 220)

½ cup Tangy Vinegar Cole Slaw (page 214)

About 1 cup pulled pork (See One-Seven Heaven Pork Shoulder, page 96)

½ cup frozen corn kernels, thawed

¼ cup chopped scallions

Pure Magic dry rub (page 29) or your choice

24 egg roll wrappers

Canola or vegetable oil, for frying

Honey Mustard Sauce (recipe follows), for serving

Combine the collards and cole slaw in a colander or strainer and drain well, but not completely. It is essential that the filling not be too wet, or the rolls will explode when they cook. But if you don't have enough liquid, then the ingredients won't bind together. You're looking for damp but not completely dry. (If the filling puddles and runs, return all the filling to a strainer and let it drain a bit more.)

(continued)
↓

Transfer the collards and slaw to a large bowl. Add the pork, corn, and scallions and mix well. Season to taste with dry rub.

Line a baking sheet with parchment paper. Place an egg roll wrapper on the work surface so it forms a diamond, with a point at the top, bottom, and sides: north, south, east, and west. Moisten just the edges of the wrapper with a little water on your finger. Scoop 2 to 3 tablespoons filling onto the middle of the wrapper, going from west to east. Fold the south corner up and over the filling, to about ½ inch below the north corner, and pull down gently to compress the filling. Seal the point. Fold the west corner over and seal, then fold over the east corner and seal. Check all of the exposed edges first and moisten with a bit more water if necessary. Tightly roll the soul roll toward the north corner, making sure it seals. Transfer the roll to the baking sheet, sealed point down. Repeat with the remaining wrappers and filling.

Line up the rolls so they aren't touching one another. Loosely cover the rolls with plastic wrap or a clean dish towel. You can fry them now, or place the baking sheet in the freezer until frozen solid and then transfer them to a freezer bag. They'll keep, frozen, for up to 3 months. When you're ready, you can cook them without thawing.

Fill a Dutch oven or large heavy-bottomed pot with the oil and heat over medium-high heat until the oil shimmers. With a slotted spoon, carefully lower the rolls, a few at a time, into the oil. Fry for 3 to 4 minutes, flipping them over once, until crispy and brown on all sides. Drain on paper towels.

Slice them on the diagonal and serve immediately with Honey Mustard Sauce.

These are much better eaten right after frying, but if you have leftovers they can be refrigerated for a few days and reheated in the oven at 375° for 8 to 10 minutes.

Variation
REUBEN SOUL ROLLS

Use scraps of pastrami to make a Reuben version.

1 cup prepared sauerkraut	2 cups finely chopped pastrami scraps	Buttermilk Russian, for dipping (recipe follows)
½ cup freshly grated Swiss cheese		

Substitute sauerkraut for the slaw and collards, add Swiss cheese, and omit the corn and scallions. Use pastrami instead of pork. Assemble and cook as directed for Soul Rolls. Serve with Buttermilk Russian instead of honey mustard sauce.

Honey Mustard Sauce

MAKES ABOUT 1¾ CUPS

Honey and brown sugar smooth the sharp edges off mustard and vinegar, resulting in a savory-sweet sauce perfect for dipping crisp meaty Soul Rolls.

¼ cup prepared yellow mustard

½ cup plus 2 tablespoons apple cider vinegar

½ cup plus 2 tablespoons packed light brown sugar

2 tablespoons ketchup (made with cane syrup, such as Red Gold or Hunt's)

2 tablespoons honey

2 tablespoons dry mustard (we use Colman's)

1 tablespoon chili powder

1 tablespoon finely ground black pepper

1¼ teaspoons kosher salt

1 teaspoon granulated garlic

Whisk all the ingredients in a small saucepan and bring to a boil, stirring constantly. Take the pan off the heat, let cool, and decant into a bowl. The sauce can be kept in a jar in the refrigerator for at least 1 week. Serve slightly warm or at room temperature.

Buttermilk Russian

MAKES ABOUT 1¾ CUPS

This dressing builds on the pickle-relish foundation of a classic Russian, but tempers the heaviness of the mayonnaise with a creamy tang from sour cream and buttermilk. Lemon juice and a touch of wing sauce give it a bright zing.

½ cup sour cream

½ cup full-fat buttermilk

¼ cup mayonnaise (we use Hellmann's)

¼ cup dill or sweet pickle relish (with no high-fructose corn syrup, such as Wickles or Cascadian Farm)

2 tablespoons ketchup (made with cane sugar, such as Red Gold or Hunt's)

1 tablespoon fresh lemon juice

2 teaspoons 17th Street Wing Sauce (page 56)

¼ teaspoon kosher salt

¼ teaspoon coarsely ground black pepper

Whisk together all the ingredients in a medium bowl. Decant into a mason jar, cover, and refrigerate; keeps for at least 2 weeks.

DEVIL'S-IN-THE-DETAILS EGGS

MAKES 24

Deviled eggs are always the first thing to disappear off the Southern buffet table. At our family gatherings, they were differentiated by garnish—bits of sweet pickle or olive, or a dash of paprika—and always displayed on a deviled egg plate made by Mama Faye at one of her ceramics classes.

This recipe is straightforward; the key is balanced flavor and a perfectly smooth filling. Be sure to taste and adjust the seasoning accordingly. Rice vinegar is smoother-tasting than other vinegars, and dusting the eggs with dry rub just before serving adds another flavor note.

12 large eggs

1½ teaspoons sugar

½ teaspoon kosher salt, plus more as needed

¼ teaspoon freshly ground black pepper

1 tablespoon rice vinegar

1 tablespoon prepared yellow mustard (such as French's)

½ teaspoon 17th Street Wing Sauce (page 56) or your favorite hot sauce

⅓ cup mayonnaise (we use Hellmann's)

Dry rub (your choice) or sweet Hungarian paprika, for garnish

Place the eggs in a large saucepan and cover with water. Bring to a boil and boil for 10 minutes. Take the pan off the heat and let sit for 5 minutes. Drain the hot water and add cold tap water to cover. Let the eggs cool completely, about 30 minutes.

Peel the eggs and halve lengthwise. Gently remove and reserve the yolks, taking care not to tear the whites. Arrange the egg whites on a baking sheet or platter and set aside.

Place the yolks in a food processor. Pulse the yolks until they completely crumble and are a fine, powder-like consistency. Add the sugar, salt, pepper, vinegar, mustard, and wing sauce. Pulse to combine. Add half the mayonnaise and blend until the mixture pulls away from the sides of the bowl. Test the consistency and add more mayonnaise to achieve the desired level of creaminess. Taste for seasoning, but don't oversalt. (The dry rub you sprinkle on at the end will add more salt flavor.) Alternatively, mix by hand: Place the yolks in a medium bowl and use a fork to crumble them. Use a whisk to blend in the remaining ingredients and add some air.

Fill a pastry bag with the filling and carefully pipe into each egg white half. Chill for 1 hour prior to serving. Sprinkle with dry rub just before serving.

BAKED VIDALIA ONION DIP

MAKES 4 CUPS

We like to say this decadent dip is a 17th Street riff on a classic French soufflé—swapping in mayo for the eggs and cream cheese for the Gruyère, and baking it in a cast-iron skillet rather than a deep fluted dish. That may or may not be true, but we suggest making a double batch—it's creamy and rich and always the first thing to go.

1½ cups chopped Vidalia onion or another sweet variety (1 large onion)

12 ounces cream cheese (1½ packages), at room temperature

1 cup finely grated Parmesan cheese

½ cup Hellmann's mayonnaise (Hellmann's makes a big difference)

2 tablespoons chopped fresh chives, for garnish

Tortilla chips, pork rinds, or club crackers, for serving

Preheat the oven to 425°, with a rack in the center.

Put the onions, cream cheese, ¾ cup of the Parmesan cheese, and the mayonnaise in a large bowl. Beat with an electric mixer on medium speed for 5 minutes or until well blended. Transfer to an 8-inch cast-iron pan or divide into smaller cast-iron pans or gratin dishes (we use small cast-iron saucepans). Don't pat the dip down into the pan; use a spatula to fluff it up. Sprinkle the remaining ¼ cup Parmesan on top.

Bake for 20 minutes, or until golden brown and bubbly on top. Do not overbake; the dip should be light and creamy. Garnish with a sprinkling of chives, and serve with tortilla chips, pork rinds, or club crackers.

BRISKET DUMPLINGS

MAKES ABOUT 50 DUMPLINGS

Andy Husbands, of the Smoke Shop in Cambridge and Tremont 647 in Boston, introduced us to this recipe when he was a guest chef and presenter at one of our OnCue catering classes. In a restaurant kitchen, we're always looking for creative ways to use leftover scraps of food that would otherwise go to waste. And as big fans of Asian dumplings, we were happy to learn how to make these and surprised by just how easy they are to assemble.

KOREAN BEEF MARINADE

½ cup light soy sauce

¼ cup packed light brown sugar

2 tablespoons honey

1 tablespoon dark sesame oil

1 tablespoon sesame seeds, toasted

1 teaspoon sriracha sauce

5 garlic cloves, smashed

5 scallions, chopped

One ½-inch piece ginger, unpeeled, sliced

KOREAN BARBECUE DIPPING SAUCE

¼ cup amber agave syrup or honey

¼ cup soy sauce

¼ cup pear or pineapple juice

2 tablespoons *gochujang* (Korean chili sauce, available in Asian markets, or see Resources, page 321)

2 teaspoons rice vinegar

2 teaspoons dark sesame oil

1 garlic clove, minced

1 teaspoon peeled and minced ginger

1 teaspoon sriracha sauce

1½ pounds cooked brisket trimmings (about 3 cups)

1 package round dumpling wrappers (usually about 50 per package)

Vegetable oil, peanut oil, or beef tallow, for frying

For the marinade: Mix all the ingredients in a small saucepan. Bring to a boil over high heat. Reduce the heat to low and simmer for 15 minutes. Take the pan off the heat and let cool to room temperature. If not using immediately, decant into a mason jar and keep in the refrigerator for up to 5 days.

For the dipping sauce: Mix all the ingredients in a small bowl. Cover and set aside until you're ready to serve.

For the dumplings: Chop the brisket trimmings. Combine with the marinade and let sit for 2 to 3 hours.

Line a baking sheet with parchment paper. Set a bowl of cold water next to it. Begin separating and arranging the dumpling wrappers in rows on the sheet. Dip your finger in water and moisten the upper half of a wrapper. Use a slotted spoon to scoop and place a tablespoon of brisket in the middle of the wrapper. Fold the bottom half up and over and press all along the edge to seal. Pick up the dumpling by the sealed edge, crimp the edges together, and return to the baking sheet. Repeat with the remaining wrappers and filling. Cover with plastic wrap and refrigerate until you're ready to cook. (Alternatively, set the baking sheet in the freezer; when the dumplings are frozen, transfer to a plastic freezer bag and keep in the freezer for up to 1 month.)

Heat 2 tablespoons vegetable oil in a large skillet over medium-high heat until shimmering. Place 6 to 10 dumplings in the pan and cook until browned, about 2 minutes per side. Pour in 1 cup water and cover the pan. Cook until the dumplings are tender, about 5 minutes. Transfer to a heatproof dish and keep warm in a low oven. Repeat with the remaining dumplings.

Alternatively, deep-fry the dumplings. Line a rimmed baking sheet with paper towels or set a wire rack on top. Add ¼ inch beef tallow or cooking oil to a Dutch oven or large heavy-bottomed pot and heat to between 325° and 350°. With a slotted spoon, carefully lower the dumplings into the oil a few at a time and fry for 2 to 3 minutes, turning once, until brown on both sides. Drain on paper towels or a wire rack.

Serve with the dipping sauce.

FREE-RANGE CHILD

By the time I was four years old, I was a regular at Barney Williams', the neighborhood grocer half a block from our house. Technically I was only supposed to go to Barney Williams' with my big sister, Jeanette, but I guess you could say I was a "free-range" child.

I was one of those kids who knew everybody in the neighborhood, and that meant everyone on my block and everyone in the surrounding blocks as well. I knew when they were baking, and I knew when to show up for the cookies. Mama Faye thought I was out playing right nearby, but really I was all over the neighborhood.

Whenever I ventured up the block to Barney Williams', I'd go down the alley, to the back door, where you had to step up to a big door that opened outward. I was too small to manage the door, so I'd knock, then step back down so Mr. Williams or Mrs. Williams or one of the clerks could open the door and see me. They knew if I showed up at the back door, I was hungry, so someone would always hand me a pig in a blanket, piping hot and held in a paper napkin.

You could get it with mustard or ketchup, and it was delicious. Mr. Williams or Mrs. Williams would pull 'em out of the oven

and sell 'em, continuously making another batch.

I'd sit right down there on the step and have a few bites, nibbling at the golden brown biscuit dough and the roasted ends of the hot dog.

I had to eat it there or finish it off walking down the alley. Either way, it had to be gone before I got back home or Mama Faye would know where I'd been. I was eventually found out when Mrs. Williams told her how cute I was. Mama Faye tried to straighten me out, telling me not to go back there alone. I didn't listen.

PIGS-IN-BLANKETS LIKE MR. AND MRS. WILLIAMS USED TO MAKE

MAKES 10

The Best Buttermilk Biscuits dough (page 236)
10 hot dogs
Ketchup and mustard

Preheat the oven to 400°, with a rack in the center. Line a baking sheet with parchment paper.

Roll out the biscuit dough as directed and cut into 3-inch circles or squares, then flatten to about ¼-inch thick with your fingers or a rolling pin. Do not overwork the dough. Roll each hot dog in dough, with both ends sticking out. Place on the baking sheet, not touching. Put the pan in the oven, lower the heat to 375°, and bake for about 10 minutes, until the dough is browned and the ends of the hot dog are browned and sizzling. Serve with ketchup or mustard.

THE KEYS TO THE KINGDOM

CLASSIC PIT-SMOKED MEATS AND MORE

THIS IS our sermon on smoke. We are here to shepherd you through the process of mastering the traditional barbecue meats—ribs, pork, brisket, and chicken. Along the way, we dispense plenty of tips and tricks, recipes and revelations, and maybe a little fire-and-brimstone testimony, too.

Our time- and pit-tested recipes for all the classic barbecue meats are broken down into a detailed, easy-to-follow, step-by-step format. You'll also go beyond the traditional basics, with chops, brats, burgers, and more.

Nothing tastes better than the barbecue you cook in your own backyard—this is as true for seasoned pros as it is for those who are new to the flame-taming game. And this, friends, is barbecue at its best.

TOOLS OF THE TRADE

We reach for these tools in our home and restaurants. See page 321 for the best places to buy them.

Brining bucket Purchase a food-grade 5-gallon brining bucket to make pastrami or porchetta. The Cambro Camwear polycarbonate square food storage container is another option. You can also purchase a roll of food-safe disposable pail liners to use with a container that might not be food safe.

Burn barrel and long-handled shovel If you're going to cook a whole hog, a burn barrel and a long-handled shovel are necessities. Burn barrels are fashioned from 55-gallon drums fitted with metal rods to hold wood, with openings cut in the top and bottom. As the wood burns, it falls to the bottom of the barrel in smaller glowing chunks, making charcoal. The charcoal is then removed through the opening in the bottom with a long-handled shovel and placed in the cooker, underneath the hog.

Cast-iron skillets, griddles, and pots Sturdy and indestructible, these can be moved from cooker to table.

Charcoal chimney Indispensable. We suggest having two so you can have one going at all times to constantly feed the fire.

Coated heat-resistant gloves To save and protect your hands when moving hot meat around the cooker.

Cutting boards Boos cutting boards are made in Effingham, Illinois, just a few hours from Murphysboro. These high-quality wooden boards will last a lifetime if you condition and care for them properly. There are many times we reach for disposable cutting boards. These make cleanup quick and easy, especially in the backyard or while traveling.

Galvanized metal trays Serving a whole hog requires something on which to present it. We have large, rectangular food-grade galvanized metal trays made for us by Voss Heating and Air Conditioning. Any local heating and air company should be able to make one since they use this material for ductwork.

GrillGrates Ridged anodized aluminum grates sit on any cooker, right on top of the existing grates, and provide flare-up protection. Invented by Brad Barrett, they conduct heat more efficiently than the grates that come with your cooker and create beautiful sear marks. We use them on the charbroilers in all of our restaurants and on our home grills, too.

Hatchet and mallet You'll need these to split the backbone if you're going to cook whole hogs.

(continued)
↓

Looftlighter Fire up that charcoal quickly with this tool.

Knives R. Murphy, the oldest family-owned handmade knife manufacturer in America, is located in Ayer, Massachusetts, and we collaborated with them on a series of carbon-steel knives. We also have a slicing knife and a butcher knife from Victorinox that we especially like. If you're going to shuck oysters, you'll need an oyster knife.

Meat grinder To make your own ground meat and sausage. The grinder attachment on a KitchenAid mixer will work well, but if you're going to start some major production, consider an LEM grinder; about $115 and up. These heavy-duty grinders are available in several capacities. The foot pedal keeps both hands free.

Meat saw For prepping hogs.

Pink butcher paper Also called peach paper, this is used for wrapping beef ribs, brisket, and pastrami to help protect and mellow the meat. We can't explain the science behind this, but it works.

Sausage stuffer This mechanism helps feed sausage meat into the casing; a necessity if you're going to make sausage.

Shakers A few of these, with varying hole sizes, are essential for storing and dispensing rub.

Oversized spatula Perfect for removing large pieces of meat from the cooker.

Squeeze bottles In a 12- to 16-ounce size, these are ideal for storing and dispensing barbecue sauces and dressings.

Spray bottles Use a heavy-duty spray bottle with an adjustable nozzle and a trigger handle to spritz meat while cooking.

String mop An old-fashioned string mop captures the most sauce and distributes it evenly over the meat.

Table and leg extenders (**PVC pipe**) A work surface that's the correct height will make a huge difference in your comfort. We keep a crate of 2-inch-diameter P.E.P. PVC pipe cut into 12- to 20-inch lengths in all of our catering vehicles and in our kitchen. Pop these on the ends of inexpensive folding tables that you can purchase at office supply stores to raise the table to a comfortable working height.

Thermometers Thermapen digital thermometers give an accurate, instant read, and they are backlit so you can see in the dark. We swear by them. If you're really getting into barbecue, invest in a more high-tech solution and get the ThermoWorks Smoke model with two probes.

Tongs Several pairs of self-locking tongs are invaluable for moving meat and vegetables around the cooker. Tongs are preferable to a fork, which will pierce the meat and allow juices to escape.

The Gospel According to Mike Mills

There is no exact recipe for barbecue. If it works for you, your friends, your family, or your customers, it's perfect. There are regional and personal preferences and subtle nuances in smoke, seasoning, and sauce—no two barbecue places taste the same, and that's a good thing. In the restaurant world, the real test is if your friends and family will buy it from you. They'll usually always eat it if it's free. The barbecue greats—the Kreuzes, Muellers, Blacks, Robinsons, Stehneys, Joneses, Monks—have all developed a clientele, both locally and from far away, who will travel to buy their barbecue. Consistency matters: today, tomorrow, and next week. In the restaurant world, inconsistency can be the death of your business. But at home, for your family and friends, is where you can have fun experimenting. Here are the governing principles by which we operate. These guidelines will help you find your way.

Temperature control is the number-one key to everything.

You'll always be managing fire throughout the cook, and there will always be variables that affect your ability to hold a steady temperature, such as the cooker itself, weather, air quality, brand of charcoal, wood, and how many times you open the cooker. Once you learn the principles of fire—how to build it slowly, what feeds it, and how to increase and decrease it when necessary—you will be able to turn out quality barbecue.

Use the lowest heat you can consistently maintain.

In our restaurants, on our large cookers, our magic temperature is 210°, which is probably the lowest in the industry. That means our meat takes longer to cook. It also means that the meat shrinks less. If you get a rack of ribs with exposed bones sticking out of the end, that means that rack of ribs was cooked at a higher temperature, causing the meat to shrink. On large-muscle meats, such as brisket and shoulder, the meat may lose half or even two-thirds its weight in shrinkage, and a little more if the heat is too high.

Consistent heat is important for the texture of the finished meat as well. Take the temperature up slowly and maintain it, instead of letting it drop and spike. If the temperature varies up and down constantly during the cook, the meat will not be as tender. **Choose a cooking temperature and stick to it.** We've given a 25° range of temperatures for all recipes in this book, but we do not mean for the temperature to fluctuate 25° throughout the cook. We want you to choose a temperature within that range and keep the cooker within 5° of that temperature at all times. For example, if the range is 225° to 250°, and you choose 230° as your target temperature, do not let the temperature dip below 225° or above 235°. This requires constant monitoring and firetending.

Charcoal is for heat, wood is for flavor.

Unless a cooker is a stick burner, charcoal is usually the heat source. Wood creates the barbecue flavor and is used in conjunction with charcoal; see Smoke Starts with Wood, page 25. We prefer sticks or chunks of wood versus wood chips, and we're not huge fans of pellet smokers. The charcoal might come from a bag or it might be coals burned down in a burn barrel and shoveled into the cooker. Some people, most notably whole hog cookers, will use only burned-down wood.

Choose your charcoal carefully.

All charcoal is not the same quality and it doesn't all give off equal heat. We prefer natural lump charcoal made by Royal Oak or competition briquets by Royal Oak or Kingsford.

Never use lighter fluid or match-light charcoal. It will impart chemical flavor to anything you cook.

Know your cooker.

You can cook good barbecue on any kind of cooker, even in a hole in the ground. I don't care if it's a 55-gallon barrel or a $10,000 pit that you had custom made. They'll all work, but you have to know what you can expect out of that piece of equipment. The key is to learn the cooker. Figure out the hot spots. Study how quickly it gets to temperature or over the desired temperature, and most important, how quickly you can take the temperature back down. You don't want to go up to 300° or 350° if you're trying to maintain 275°. That variation in temperature has a tremendous effect on the quality and texture of your end product. Learn where to put the coals or add coals so you can maintain an even temperature.

Before cooking any meat on a new pit, use the old-standby canned biscuit test. Prepare a fire with an indirect cooking area in the cooker, as though you are going to cook meat, and arrange the biscuits on the indirect side. Check the biscuits every 5 minutes. Pay attention to which ones get darker and also how they rise. This exercise shows you the hot spots on your cooker; that information will be important as you arrange and rotate your meat during a cook. A rundown on our favorite cookers is opposite.

OUR FAVORITE COOKERS

We've had dozens of cookers of the years and here are the ones we use at home. See the Resources section (page 321) for purchasing information. If you buy a grill (such as a Weber, Primo, Hasty Bake, or PK Grill) to do double-duty as a smoker, make sure it has a hinged grate to make it easier to add coals and wood during cooking. For a selection of our favorite pits for cooking whole hog, see page 323.

Ole Hickory Ace MM The MM stands for Mike Mills, and this model is a premium piece of equipment for the super enthusiast. A home or competition version of the large cookers we use in our restaurants, this charcoal- and wood-burning insulated cooker has a built-in fan system. With 19.51 square feet of cooking space, it is so well insulated that it will hold a specified temperature for up to 6 hours. It's designed to not go above 275°.

Cowboy Cauldron These impressive cauldrons also double as fire pits and really look great in your backyard. Designed for live-fire cooking, you can smoke on these simply by using a lid from a kettle cooker.

Primo Kamado Ceramic cookers are available at varying price points and quality. We particularly like the Primo because its oval shape offers more usable cooking area than a round cooker. Primo uses the highest grade of ceramic available and their cookers offer superior heat, moisture retention, and temperature control. These lifetime pieces of equipment are low maintenance, and they're made to live outdoors.

Weber Summit Charcoal Series This new model has all the bells and whistles. There's a firing mechanism so you don't have to use a charcoal chimney, an adjustable hinged grate, and all sorts of extras. The real selling point is that it's insulated with air, so you can take the heat down much more easily than you can with any other cooker.

Red Box Smoker Small and affordable, this insulated, double-walled, reverse-flow smoker is perfect for the terrace or deck of an apartment or as an addition to your cooker arsenal. Don't let the size fool you, though. The three racks can accommodate four slabs of ribs, two small brisket flats, two Boston butts, or three split chickens.

Pit Barrel Cooker Affordable and easy to use, this 30-gallon drum cooks consistently good barbecue via the hanging method. The meat is suspended in the center of the heat, allowing even cooking and a smoky fog created by the juices that drip directly on the coals. A grate attachment lets you cook steaks and burgers. The barrel is coated with porcelain enamel to make it durable and weather resistant.

Take extra care in prepping meat.

We eat with our eyes first, and first appearances, no matter where I am, are important to me. I want you to be able to eat an entire rack of ribs down to the bone, without removing any undesirable piece from your mouth, and I don't want people to have to struggle with hunks of fat or gristle in a sandwich. We take off the membrane on pork and beef ribs and trim off any extraneous fat that won't render during the cooking process. Even if we're at an event where we're cooking a pallet of ribs, we still take the time to examine and trim every single rack.

Consistent weight is important.

If you're cooking multiple pieces of meat, try to keep their weights the same. If one rack of ribs, for example, weighs 2 pounds and another weighs 3 pounds, they'll be done at different times. Never assume if one piece is done, they're all done. Even when two pieces of meat weigh the same, the structure of the meat can vary, and each piece can take a different amount of time to thoroughly cook. You have to feel and/or take the temperature of each piece of meat.

Size matters.

Portion the meat into manageable pieces that fit properly on the cooker. Depending upon what size cooker you're working with, you can cut racks of ribs in halves or thirds, separate the point and flat on a brisket, or portion butts into smaller pieces. Cook chicken or turkey in pieces if you can't comfortably fit a whole bird. This allows the meat to cook in less time and gives you even more control over grill space.

Start with cold meat.

Put the meat on the cooker when it's cold. Meat takes on smoke until it reaches an internal temperature of about 140°, so putting it on cold and controlling the rise of temperature allows it to cook slowly and begin breaking down the connective tissue, while taking in the proper amount of smoke. After 140°, smoke will begin accumulating on the outside of the meat. That's when meat gets oversmoked and tastes acrid.

Use a mustard slather.

On large-muscle cuts and those without a sufficient layer of external fat, we like to use a mustard slather (page 31), which doesn't add flavor as it mostly cooks away, but helps the rub adhere to the meat and provides a layer of protection.

Black bark is beautiful on a butt or a brisket.

When we see black bark on large-muscle meats—a butt, shoulder, or brisket—we know we've taken that smoke flavor through the meat, and that's a good thing. But on smaller, thinner cuts of meat, such as ribs and poultry, a rich mahogany color is more desirable; black usually means the meat is burned. Meat blackens when you've used too much rub, or had heavy bark on the wood you used to smoke, or if your heat was too high.

Meat should not fall off the bone.

The meat should be tender, but have some structure and not turn to mush. With a pork rib, for example, you should be able to take a clean bite and feel a little tug. You don't want the meat to fall off or come completely away from the bone. That means the meat is overcooked or has been foiled for too long.

Don't use aluminum foil.

Wrapping ribs in foil to help achieve tenderness is advocated by a number of barbecue authors. I'm against this practice. I jokingly say, "I *used* to wrap my ribs, until I learned how to cook 'em right." Simmering ribs in a foil packet, filled with apple juice or other liquid, essentially removes all of the smoke flavor you so carefully infused, and it can turn the ribs to mush very quickly. If you learn to manage the fire, you'll never have to use foil.

Invest in an accurate thermometer.

A Thermapen digital thermometer (see page 76) costs $60 to $100, but when you're investing your time and efforts into what you're cooking, that's a small price to pay for dead-on accuracy.

It's done when it's done.

Barbecue is an art, not a science. There is no hard-and-fast rule dictating a set cooking temperature or length of cooking time that will deliver perfectly cooked barbecue. Every piece of meat, every piece of equipment, every fire is different. In the barbecue recipes in this book, we've given you some ranges of cook time on page 86, but these are guesstimates.

Measure doneness by temperature and by feel.

When the meat is done, the thermometer should glide in as though it's sliding into a warm stick of butter. If it hits a hard spot, then hits another, the meat is probably okay to eat but isn't properly cooked and isn't quite as tender as it should be. This is a major mistake most people make. They go by the temperature and don't account for the structure of the meat itself. Sometimes just 20 or 30 minutes more will mean the difference between a good piece of barbecue and a great one. For ribs, we go strictly by feel.

Don't keep opening the cooker.

When you're taking the temperature of the meat, you want to be in and out of the cooker quickly. There's a reason for the old saying, "If you're lookin', you're not cookin'." Every time you lift up the lid, you add 15 to 20 minutes to your cooking time. After enough practice, you will become confident enough so that you know what is going on inside that cooker.

Know the ambient temperature of the cooker at all times.

There are always two temperatures to consider inside the cooker—the ambient temperature and the temperature of the meat itself.

The built-in thermometers on charcoal cookers and grills are notoriously inaccurate. Even the high-end cookers, such as the Primo and the Weber Summit, provide readings that, while more trustworthy, tell you what the temperature is near the sensor rather than down where the meat is, which is much closer to the hot coals and can therefore be 20° to 30° higher than up near the thermometer.

Solutions: Option one is to use your Thermapen (see page 76) to measure the temperature in the top part of the cooker, near the built-in thermometer, by sticking the probe down through the exhaust vent at the top of your cooker.

Note that temperature. Then measure the temperature at the grate level, where the meat is sitting. Hold the Thermapen just above the grate. That's the important temperature. Place the probe of the Thermapen inside the cooker and close the lid, so the end where you read the temperature is sticking outside. Note the difference in that temperature and the one taken at the top of the pit. If you're going to rely on the built-in thermometer, always remember to make a mental adjustment for the real temperature near the meat.

Option two is to go a little more high tech and get yourself a ThermoWorks Smoke. This kit allows you to simultaneously measure the temperature of a piece of meat and the ambient temperature of your cooker. And it does it remotely, no less, using a portable monitor. At $99, you get a big bang for your buck.

THE POWER OF TELEVISION

Barbecue television shows have helped raise awareness of the barbecue competition world and have made food personalities out of some of barbecue's most powerful competition cookers. We in the industry are grateful for this exposure, but it means that we have to keep educating people about the difference between competition barbecue and the barbecue you find in restaurants or the kind you want to cook in your own backyard. Much of our reputation was formed on the competition circuit and we've hosted our own contest in Murphysboro for over thirty years. What has happened, though, is that the flavor profile necessary to win a competition has become very sweet, and the methods you have to use to get the tenderness and flavor profile necessary to win are sometimes at odds with the principles behind barbecue. Judges are taking just one bite of each entry, so that bite has to be a burst of flavor. If you ate an entire serving of some competition barbecue, you'd probably have a stomachache. Cooking-wise, ribs are covered with honey or agave syrup and apple juice, and wrapped with foil and simmered to achieve a specific tenderness; chicken is poached in butter in a cupcake tin, among other techniques. All of these methods produce prize-winning entries, but this is not the barbecue you'll want to replicate at home.

TEMPERATURE GUIDE*

Cut	Weight	Timing	Temperature of meat when cooked
Baby back ribs	2 to 2½ pounds	3 to 5 hours	The rack will bend when you pick up one end and the meat will pull away from the bone. If the fire's too hot, the meat will shrink and expose bone on the sides.
St. Louis–style ribs	2¼ to 3-plus pounds	4 to 6 hours	
Pork shoulder	15 to 18 pounds	12 to 18 hours	185° to 190° to pull, 175° to 180° to slice
Boston butt	8 to 10 pounds	8 to 12 hours	185° to 190° to pull, 175° to 180° to slice
Ham	14 to 16 pounds	2 to 3 hours	143° to 145°
Pork loin	8 to 10 pounds	3 to 4 hours	150° to 155°
Beef ribs	7 to 8 pounds	4 to 6 hours	185° to 190° wrapped; 195° to 200° not wrapped
Beef brisket, whole	12 to 16 pounds	14 to 18 hours	185° to 190°
Beef tenderloin	5 to 6 pounds	3 to 4 hours	130° for rare; 135° for medium-rare; 145° for medium
Prime rib	13 to 14 pounds	3½ to 4½ hours	110° to 115° for rare; 118° to 120° medium
Chicken	2½ to 3 pounds	1½ to 2 hours	165°
	3½ to 4½ pounds	3 to 4 hours	165°
Turkey (split breast)	7 to 8 pounds	3 hours	165°

One of our secrets is very simple. Other books will tell you to cook at higher temperatures, but we're truly low and slow. If we're cooking on an Ole Hickory, we keep the cooker temperature between 210° and 225° for everything we cook, except chicken. For chicken, we raise the temperature to between 240° and 250°. When we're cooking on a grill meant for home use, it's hard to keep the temperature that low. We might go up to between 250° and 275°. Lower heat gives us time to get a deep penetration of flavor and creates less shrinkage in the meat.

*For larger cuts of meat, temperatures indicate when to take the meat off the cooker; internal temperature will continue to rise while the meat rests.

(OPPOSITE) Pork shoulder, flipped over, showing the seasoning and grill marks on the cooking side.

LEGENDARY BABY BACK RIBS

MAKES 3 FULL-RACK SERVINGS OR 6 HALF-RACK SERVINGS

Our royalty status on the competition circuit originated with our long-reigning champion baby back ribs. Also known as loin backs, baby backs are cut "high on the hog" and come from the curved region of the rib cage. You'll notice the bones have a slight arch to them, and the meat has a bit of pork chop or pork loin flavor. When buying your baby backs, pay attention to the size of the ribs. We prefer smaller 2-pound racks, which come off a younger hog and are more tender, with a higher meat-to-bone ratio.

The other secret to delicious ribs—of any cut—is cooking them long enough. Because there's not enough meat on a rib to easily use a thermometer, rib doneness is best checked by hand: Lift up the rack, using one finger, from one end; it should bend like a swayback horse. If it doesn't bend much or has any tension at all, it needs to go back on the cooker. If you cut the rack in half or thirds, you'll be able to pick up the pieces individually and bend them in order to judge doneness. They should bend easily, but not break in half. When you've cooked enough racks, you'll be an expert judge of perfect doneness. Meantime, be patient.

Experiment with different combinations of rubs and sauces, from savory to sweet, to give the ribs a whole different flavor.

3 racks baby back ribs (about 2 pounds each)	Apple City Barbecue Sauce (page 36) or Blackberry-Habanero Sauce (page 37), warm	4 to 5 pounds good-quality lump charcoal
Pure Magic (page 29) or Sweet Heat Dry Rub (page 33)		1 small (8-inch) piece of apple wood or 2 store-bought chunks
2 cups apple juice in a spray bottle with a trigger handle (see page 76)		String mop (see page 76)

Prep the meat: To remove the thin, papery membrane from the inner side of the ribs, lay each rack, bone side up, on a flat surface and slide the handle of a teaspoon between the membrane and the meat, working from one end all the way to the other. Use a paper towel to grab ahold of the membrane and pull firmly to peel the whole thing off. Then use the bowl end of the spoon to scrape away any extraneous fat on the bone side of the rack, between the bones. Don't scrape all the way down to the bone; just remove any thick deposits. Turn the rack over and

inspect the front. Use a sharp knife to trim off any scraggly edges and hard pieces of fat (which won't render out during the cooking process).

Cut the racks in halves or thirds as needed to fit on the cooker. Lightly sprinkle each side with dry rub. You'll be layering on rub several times during the cooking process, so don't overdo it now. Set the ribs on a baking sheet, cover them with plastic wrap, and refrigerate until you're ready to put them on the cooker.

Note: You can dust the ribs with dry rub up to 4 hours prior to cooking, but if they sit much longer than that, the salt in the rub will begin to pull moisture from the meat.

Set up the cooker for indirect-heat smoking: Open the top and bottom vents. Pile 3 pounds of the charcoal in one half of the cooker, leaving the other half empty. Load a charcoal chimney one-quarter full of charcoal and light it. When the coals in the chimney are glowing, dump them on top of the pile of charcoal in the cooker. Set the wood on top of the coals, replace the grate, and put the ribs over the side with no coals (the indirect cooking area), bone side down. Close the lid.

Don't open the cooker for 1 hour, but keep a close eye on the temperature (see page 84 for how best to assess and monitor cooker temperature); when it reaches 185°, which might happen very quickly, close the vents about halfway so that less air comes in to feed the fire and the heat in the cooker rises slowly. Let the temperature climb to between 225° and 250° (see page 77 for how to determine your target temperature). **Maintain your target temperature for the duration of the cook.**

Throughout the entirety of the cook, be on the lookout for fluctuations in cooker temperature; if it dips more than 5° below your target and opening the vents isn't sufficient to bring it back up, you will need to add a few hot coals. If at any point the temperature climbs above your target by more than 5°, close the top and bottom vents further so that even less air comes in to feed the fire.

After 1 hour, open the lid and check the edges of the ribs closest to the fire. If they look like they're beginning to brown, rotate the racks, moving the pieces that are farthest away and placing them closest to the fire, and vice versa. (Do not flip the ribs over, now or at any other point during the cook.)

Close the lid and continue cooking the ribs for another 2 to 4 hours, monitoring the cooker temperature and checking every 20 minutes or so to see if the surface of the meat looks dry or moist. If the ribs look dry, mist them with some apple juice and sprinkle on another light coat of dry rub. Ribs "sweat" about three times during the smoking process, indicating that the seasoning from the dry rub and the flavor from the smoke are being absorbed into the meat. Never flip the ribs over; instead continue rotating them so each piece cooks evenly.

Prepare another round of charcoal in the chimney as needed. This cook should not require more charcoal than the initial amount, but we always keep some coals at the ready just in case more are needed to maintain the temperature.

After the ribs have been on the cooker for 3 hours, start checking every 20 minutes or so for doneness by lifting up one end of a rack. If the rack is still rigid like a board or bends only a little, the ribs need more time. When they're done, the rack will sway, bending in the middle.

Mop the ribs with a thin coat of sauce, then close the lid for just a minute to let it dry a bit. Mop with a second thin coat, give them a final sprinkle of dry rub, pull them off the cooker, and serve. Serve full or half racks, or cut into single or double bones to serve as an appetizer.

MEAT ME IN ST. LOUIS RIBS

MAKES 3 FULL-RACK SERVINGS OR 6 HALF-RACK SERVINGS

The term "St. Louis rib" has nothing to do with a cooking style or flavor profile—it refers to the way the meat is butchered: cut from the center of the spare ribs, which is the large, flat area from the flat belly side of a hog. Whereas baby back ribs have a pork chop flavor, the St. Louis cut tastes more like bacon, since it's from the belly. As with baby backs, we prefer smaller ribs, which may be difficult to find, but most meat departments or specialty stores can help you out with special ordering. It's (literally) worth noting that St. Louis ribs cost significantly less per pound than baby backs. If we hadn't made our name cooking baby backs, we'd be all about St. Louis ribs at our restaurant.

3 racks St. Louis cut pork ribs (2¼ to 2½ pounds each)

Basic Dry Rub (page 33) or your choice

2 cups apple juice in a spray bottle with a trigger handle (see page 76)

Raspberry-Chipotle Sauce (page 38) or your choice, warm

4 to 5 pounds good-quality lump charcoal

1 small (8-inch) piece of apple wood or 2 store-bought chunks

String mop (see page 76)

Prep the meat: To remove the thin, papery membrane from the inner side of the ribs, lay each rack, bone side up, on a flat surface and slide the handle of a teaspoon between the membrane and the meat, working from one end all the way to the other. Use a paper towel to grab ahold of the membrane and pull firmly to peel the whole thing off. Then use the bowl end of the spoon to scrape away any extraneous fat on the bone side of the rack, between the bones. Don't scrape all the way down to the bone, just remove any thick deposits. Turn the rack over and inspect the front. Use a sharp knife to trim off any scraggly edges and hard pieces of fat (which won't render out during the cooking process).

Cut the racks in halves or thirds as needed to fit on the cooker. Lightly sprinkle each side with dry rub. You'll be layering on rub several times during the cooking process, so don't overdo it now. Set the ribs on a baking sheet, cover them with plastic wrap, and refrigerate until you're ready to put them on the cooker.

Note: You can dust the ribs with dry rub up to 4 hours prior to cooking, but if they sit much longer than that, the salt in the rub will begin to pull moisture from the meat.

(continued)

↓

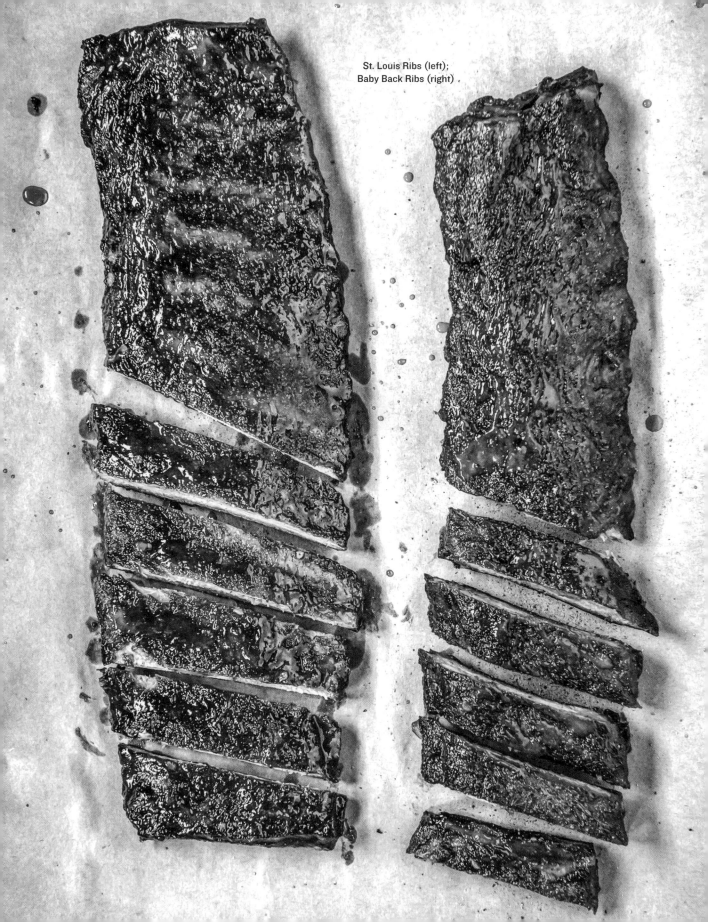

St. Louis Ribs (left);
Baby Back Ribs (right)

Set up the cooker for indirect cooking: Open the top and bottom vents. Pile 3 pounds of the charcoal in one half of the cooker, leaving the other half empty. Load a charcoal chimney one-quarter full of charcoal and light it. When the coals in the chimney are glowing, dump them on top of the pile of charcoal in the cooker. Set the wood on top of the coals, replace the grate, and put the ribs over the side with no coals (the indirect cooking area), bone side down. Close the lid.

Don't open the cooker for 1 hour, but keep a close eye on the temperature (see page 84 for how best to assess and monitor cooker temperature); when it reaches 185°, which might happen very quickly, close the vents about halfway so that less air comes in to feed the fire and the heat in the cooker rises slowly. Let the temperature climb to between 225° and 250° (see page 77 for how to determine your target temperature). **Maintain your target temperature for the duration of the cook.**

Throughout the entirety of the cook, be on the lookout for fluctuations in cooker temperature; if it dips more than 5° below your target and opening the vents isn't sufficient to bring it back up, you will need to add a few hot coals. If at any point the temperature climbs above your target by more than 5°, close the top and bottom vents even more so that even less air comes in to feed the fire.

After 1 hour, open the lid and check the edges of the ribs closest to the fire. If they look like they're beginning to brown, rotate the racks, moving the pieces that are farthest away and placing them closest to the fire, and vice versa. (Do not flip the ribs over, now or at any other point during the cook.)

Close the lid and continue smoking the ribs for another 2 to 4 hours, monitoring the cooker temperature and checking every 20 minutes or so to see if the surface of the meat looks dry or moist. If the ribs look dry, mist them with some apple juice and sprinkle on another light coat of dry rub. Ribs "sweat" about three times during the smoking process, indicating that the seasoning from the dry rub and the flavor from the smoke are being absorbed into the meat. Never flip the ribs over; instead continue rotating them so each rack cooks evenly.

Prepare another round of charcoal in the chimney as needed. This cook should not require more charcoal than the initial amount, but we always keep some coals at the ready just in case more are needed to maintain the temperature.

After the ribs have been on the cooker for 3 hours, start checking for doneness every 20 minutes or so by lifting up one end of a rack. If the rack is still rigid like a board or bends only a little, the ribs need more time. When they're done the rack will sway, bending in the middle.

Mop the ribs with a thin coat of sauce, then close the lid for just a minute to let it dry a bit. Mop with a second thin coat, give them a final sprinkle of dry rub, pull them off the cooker, and serve. Serve full or half racks, or cut into single or double bones to serve as an appetizer.

ONE-SEVEN HEAVEN PORK SHOULDER

A SHOULDER WILL YIELD 9 TO 12 USABLE POUNDS OF MEAT; A BUTT, 5 TO 7 POUNDS (1 POUND OF COOKED PORK IS ENOUGH FOR 4 TO 6 SANDWICHES)

Whole pork shoulder has two components: the shank or picnic, which is the bottom third of the shoulder, including the shank bone; and the butt (or Boston butt), which is the top two thirds of the shoulder, including the blade bone. Cooking the entire shoulder gets you maximum flavor because it incorporates meat from a variety of muscles, but if you need to operate on a smaller scale, you can certainly opt for either. All told, depending upon the weight of the meat and the cooking temperature, a whole pork shoulder can take upward of 12 hours; a butt can take 8 hours or more.

Proper prep is essential. The shoulder will still have part of the hide attached, which needs to be peeled back so that you can season the fat underneath, then put back in place to protect the meat during the cook. On the rest of the shoulder, the thick areas of fat need to be trimmed down to ¼ to ⅜ inch, because thicker fat will not render and will act as a barrier, preventing smoke from penetrating the meat. Also, you need to feel around for and remove hard pieces of fat because they won't render out during the cook. Careful prep is well worth the time and work it takes, as it ensures the interior of the shoulder will be deeply infused with smoky flavor while the exterior develops a luscious bark. The goal is a deep dark bark; "blond" is too light, and a sign of insufficient smoke.

Mind the distinction between shoulder that will be sliced versus pulled: The meat is cooked to different internal temperatures, and needs to be a little firmer for slicing.

Cooking and serving traditions vary widely. In western North Carolina barbecue restaurants, shoulder is served cubed, sliced, and pulled, all on one plate. In Southern Illinois and southeast Missouri, there is a long tradition of the sliced barbecue pork shoulder sandwich. Here in Murphysboro, a nearly century-old tradition in barbecue restaurants that have come and gone is to serve a sort of barbecue panini: a sliced pork sandwich griddled under a foil-covered brick and topped with Chow (page 217). We call our 17th Street rendition the One-7 Slice of Heaven (17th Street is known among Murphysboro locals as "The One-7").

(continued)

↓

One 15- to 18-pound bone-in pork shoulder or an 8- to 10-pound bone-in butt

Dry rub (your choice)

Mustard Slather (page 31)

FOR SANDWICHES

Hog Wash Vinegar Splash (page 40) in a squirt bottle

Potato rolls or squishy white bread

Barbecue sauce (your choice) in a squirt bottle

Tangy Vinegar Cole Slaw (page 214) or Chow (page 217)

Butter (optional)

15 pounds good-quality lump charcoal

2 small (8-inch) pieces of apple wood or 4 store-bought chunks

Foil-covered brick (optional)

Prep the meat: For a shoulder, season underneath the hide covering the exterior side. Use a sharp, flexible boning knife to cut around the edges and up underneath the hide, up to the end where it is attached to the shank bone, then pull the hide away from the shoulder like a curtain (it will be attached at the top). This will expose a layer of fat. Season the fat with dry rub and pull the hide back over it. This will protect the meat as it cooks. On the opposite side of the shoulder, trim all the visible areas of fat down to ¼ to ⅜ inch. Run your fingers over the meat, feeling for hard pieces of fat; cut these pieces away. Also remove any visible veins. On a butt, one side will be thickly clad with fat; leave this fat cap untrimmed. Trim the fat on the opposite side of the butt as instructed for the non-hide side of the shoulder.

At least 20 minutes before putting the meat on the cooker, coat all of the exposed meat, but not the hide, with a thin layer of Mustard Slather and sprinkle generously with dry rub. Set the meat on a rimmed baking sheet, loosely cover with plastic wrap, and refrigerate until you're ready to put it on the cooker.

Note: You can dust the pork with dry rub up to 4 hours prior to cooking, but if it sits much longer than that, the salt in the rub will begin to pull moisture from the meat.

Set up the cooker for indirect-heat smoking: Open the top and bottom vents. Pile 3 pounds of the charcoal in one half of the cooker, leaving the other half empty. Load a charcoal chimney one-quarter full of charcoal and light it. When the coals in the chimney are glowing, dump them on top of the pile of charcoal already in the cooker. Set half the wood on top of the coals, replace the grate, and put the meat on the cooker, over the side with no coals (the indirect cooking area), skin side up for a shoulder, bone-side down and fat side up for a butt.

Keep a close eye on the temperature (see page 84 for how best to assess and monitor cooker temperature); when it reaches 200°, which might happen very quickly, close the vents about halfway so that less air comes in to feed the fire and the heat in the cooker rises slowly. Let the temperature climb to between 250° and 275° (see page 77 for how to determine your target temperature). **Maintain your target temperature for the duration of the cook.**

Throughout the entirety of the cook, be on the lookout for fluctuations in cooker temperature; whenever it dips more than 5° and opening the vents isn't sufficient to bring it back up, it's time to add a few hot coals from the chimney. You'll need to prepare another round of charcoal every few hours as needed. If at any point the temperature climbs above your target by more than 5°, close the top and bottom vents further so that even less air comes in to feed the fire.

After the pork has been on the cooker for 3 hours, periodically check the edges of the meat closest to the fire. Rotate the meat as needed to brown evenly, but never flip it over. Use an instant-read thermometer to check the temperature of the meat: Insert the probe into the middle, without touching the bone; you're looking for a slow and steady climb toward 190°. As the wood burns throughout the cook, continue to add the other pieces until the internal temperature of the meat reaches between 135° and 140°. The meat may get very dark or even blacken; for pork shoulder that is a good thing.

When the internal temperature of the meat reaches 175° to 180° for slicing or 185° to 190° for pulling, take the pork off the cooker and set it on a cutting board to rest for 20 to 30 minutes prior to removing the bone.

Remove the bone by sliding your fingers down along each side, grabbing a hold of it and twisting the bone side to side to loosen and pull it out. If the pork is done and tender, the bone should slide right out. If you've cooked the meat to the lower temperature for slicing, the bone will be more difficult to remove; insert a flexible boning knife and run it around the edges of the bone before trying to pull it out. Remove and discard the hide and any large chunks of fat or gristle.

For pulled pork, break the meat apart with your hands, then chop with a cleaver or put it in a 5-gallon bucket and use a Porkinator (see Resources, page 321). Liberally squirt Hog Wash over the meat and fluff with your hands to combine. Sprinkle with some dry rub and fluff again.

To build a pulled pork sandwich, mound a pile of meat on a bottom bun and sprinkle with a little more dry rub. Working from the outside in, squirt a stream of barbecue sauce along the edge, working your way toward the middle in a spiral; this makes for a bit of barbecue sauce in each bite. Top with slaw, then the other half of the bun, and serve. Freeze leftover pulled pork in freezer bags, taking care to squeeze out all the air before sealing, for up to 2 months.

(continued)

↓

For sliced pork, thinly slice the meat about ⅛ inch thick with a very sharp carving knife. Cut only as much as you need for sandwiches or to serve immediately. Wrap the remainder tightly with plastic wrap until you're ready to slice more. Alternatively, slice the entire piece of meat and wrap individual 4- to 6-ounce servings in plastic wrap, then package in freezer bags.

To make a Murphysboro-style barbecue pork sandwich, layer 3 or 4 slices of pork on a bottom bun and sprinkle with a little dry rub. Working from the outside in, squirt a stream of barbecue sauce along the edge, working your way inward in a concentric spiral; this makes for a bit of barbecue sauce in each bite. Top with the other half of the bun. Melt a tablespoon of butter in a heavy skillet and toast the sandwich on one side until browned. Flip the sandwich over and add another tablespoon of butter if necessary. Set a foil-covered brick on top of the sandwich and griddle it until the bottom is browned and the sandwich is pressed. Lift the top bun and add a spoonful of slaw or chow. Slice in half and serve.

CARAMELIZED MIDWEST PORK STEAKS

MAKES 4 TO 6 SERVINGS

Pork steak is a Midwest classic that most home cooks just grill, which is a fine way to get good outdoor flavor from an inexpensive cut of meat. But we give ours a special reverse-sear treatment: first dusting the steaks lightly with dry rub, then infusing with the gentle smoke of apple wood, next grilling, and finally mopping with sauce and caramelizing them over direct fire.

As commonplace as they are in the Midwest, pork steaks are not usually found in grocery meat cases elsewhere, but obtaining them is as easy as asking your butcher to cut them from the butt end of a pork shoulder—specify 1-inch-thick steaks that weigh about a pound apiece, since this is the optimal size for taking on smoke. The steaks can be smoked a day or two in advance and finished on the grill just prior to serving. You can even freeze a pile of smoked steaks for up to 1 month, then pull them out, thaw, and grill them as needed.

4 to 6 bone-in pork steaks (about 1 pound each)

Pure Magic dry rub (page 29) or your choice

Apple City Barbecue Sauce (page 36), or your choice, warm

1 to 3 pounds good-quality lump charcoal

1 small (8-inch) piece of apple wood or 2 store-bought chunks

String mop (see page 76)

Lightly sprinkle the pork steaks with dry rub on both sides. Set the steaks on a baking sheet, cover them with plastic wrap, and refrigerate until you're ready to put them on the cooker.

Note: You can dust the steaks with dry rub up to 4 hours prior to cooking, but if the steaks sit any longer than that, the salt in the rub will begin to pull moisture from the meat.

Set up the cooker for indirect-heat smoking: Open the top and bottom vents. Load a charcoal chimney one-quarter full of charcoal and light it. When the coals in the chimney are glowing, dump them on one side of the cooker. Set the wood on top of the coals, replace the grate, and put the steaks over the side with no coals (the indirect cooking area). Close the lid.

(continued)

↓

Don't open the cooker for 15 minutes, but keep a close eye on the temperature (see page 84 for how best to assess and monitor cooker temperature); when it reaches 200°, which might happen very quickly, close the vents about halfway so that less air comes in to feed the fire and the heat in the cooker rises slowly. Let the temperature climb to between 225° and 250° (see page 77 for how to determine your target temperature). **Maintain your target temperature;** if at any point it climbs above your target, close the top and bottom vents further so that even less air comes in to feed the fire.

After 15 minutes, use an instant-read thermometer to check the internal temperature of the meat: Insert the probe into the center of one of the steaks, not near the bone. You are looking for a slow and steady climb to between 160° and 165°. Do not flip the steaks over at all during the smoking stage.

After you check the meat temperature, reload the chimney halfway with charcoal and light it. You'll soon need these additional hot coals to sear the steaks at the finishing stage, after they're done smoking.

Check the internal temperature of the meat every 10 minutes or so. When the steaks are between 160° and 165°, pull them off the cooker and set them aside on a baking sheet. Working quickly, add the hot coals, spreading them out all over the bottom of the cooker. Lightly mop the tops of the steaks with the barbecue sauce, sprinkle on a light layer of dry rub, and put the steaks back on the cooker, sauce side down, directly over the hot coals. Cook the steaks for 5 to 8 minutes, mopping with the sauce and flipping them several times to caramelize all over. If there are spots of fat that are dark and blackened, sauce them and caramelize them again. When the steaks are sizzling around the bone and beautifully glazed on both sides and around the edges, they're done. The internal temperature should be between 170° and 175°.

BOURBON-BUTTERED REVERSE-SEAR DOUBLE-CUT PORK CHOPS

MAKES 4 TO 6 SERVINGS

Heritage-breed pork chops cooked in the reverse-sear method are amazingly tender, juicy, and flavorful. Cooking pork chops to white is a sin; pink is perfect and an internal temperature between 150° and 155° is ideal.

4 to 6 bone-in pork chops (¾ to 1 pound each, 1½ to 2 inches thick; preferably Duroc or another heritage breed)	Steakhouse Shake (page 32) Top-Shelf Bourbon Butter (page 241), chilled, for serving	2 pounds good-quality lump charcoal 2 small (8-inch) pieces of apple wood or 3 or 4 store-bought chunks

Up to 40 minutes prior to cooking, generously sprinkle the chops with shake on both sides. Set the chops on a baking sheet, cover them with plastic wrap, and refrigerate until you're ready to put them on the cooker.

Set up the cooker for indirect-heat smoking: Open the top and bottom vents. Load a charcoal chimney one-quarter full of charcoal and light it. When the coals in the chimney are glowing, dump them on one side of the cooker. Set the wood on top of the coals, replace the grate, and put the chops over the side with no coals (the indirect cooking area). Close the lid.

Don't open the cooker for 15 minutes, but keep a close eye on the temperature (see page 84 for how best to assess and monitor cooker temperature); when it reaches 200°, which might happen very quickly, close the vents about halfway so that less air comes in to feed the fire and the heat in the cooker rises slowly. Let the temperature climb to between 225° and 250° (see page 77 for how to determine your target temperature). **Maintain your target temperature.** If at any point the temperature climbs above your target, close the top and bottom vents further so that even less air comes in to feed the fire.

After 15 minutes, open the cooker and use an instant-read thermometer to check the internal temperature of the thickest part of a chop; you're looking for a slow and steady climb to 145°. This will take no longer than 30 minutes.

After you check the meat temperature, reload the chimney halfway with charcoal and light it. You'll soon need these additional hot coals to sear the chops at the finishing stage, after they're done smoking.

When the chops reach 145°, set them aside on a baking sheet. Working quickly, add the hot coals and spread them out all over the bottom of the cooker. Replace the grate and put the chops back on the cooker. Sear for a minute or two on each side, just until a brown crust forms and the internal temperature is between 150° and 155°. Pull the chops off the cooker, top each with a slice of bourbon butter, and serve.

LONE STAR BEEF RIBS

MAKES 4 TO 8 SERVINGS

Renowned Texas pit masters the likes of Wayne Mueller and John Lewis have elevated the classic Texas–style beef ribs to iconic status. Little flurries of fat and marbling throughout the meat make for rich flavor and unrivaled melt-in-your-mouth tenderness, punctuated with spicy bursts of pepper from the gorgeously crusty bark.

Beef ribs come in 3- or 4-bone sections, and they weigh somewhere in the neighborhood of 7 to 8 pounds per section. There will be some shrinkage during the cooking process; the finished rack will end up weighing 3 to 4 pounds. Just like pork ribs, there are different cuts of ribs butchered from a cow—back, plate, and chuck ribs. We like to use the plate ribs, but the chuck ribs are sometimes easier to find and a little less expensive. They're often labeled simply "short ribs."

Outside of Texas, this can be a hard cut to find. Request them from your butcher or mail-order from Snake River Farms (see Resources, page 321).

Pitmasters judge the doneness of their beef ribs by pressing the meat with a finger—if it goes in up to the first knuckle, it's done. But until you're very experienced, it's best to use an instant-read thermometer. Unlike baby backs, beef ribs are meaty enough to check this way, and you'll know they're done both by the temperature (between 195° and 210°) and by the way the thermometer probe slides in smoothly, like you're poking it into a stick of butter.

One 7- to 8-pound rack beef ribs (prime or choice grade)	15 pounds good-quality lump charcoal	25- to 38-quart insulated cooler, large enough to fit the meat with room to spare (not Styrofoam or vinyl—we use Igloo, Rubbermaid, or Yeti; optional)
Mustard Slather (page 31)	3 small (8-inch) pieces of post oak or 6 store-bought chunks	
Texas Forever Brisket Rub (page 30)	Pink butcher paper (optional; see page 76)	

Prep the meat: Remove any membrane from the back of the rack, especially if there's a heavy sheathing, and use a spoon to scrape off any excess fat. Coat the entire rack of ribs with a thin layer of Mustard Slather and sprinkle generously with dry rub. Put the rack on a baking sheet, loosely cover with plastic wrap, and refrigerate until you're ready to put it on the cooker.

(continued)
↓

Note: You can apply the rub to the ribs up to 4 hours prior to cooking, but if they sit much longer than that, the salt in the rub will begin to pull moisture from the meat.

Set up the cooker for indirect-heat smoking: Open the top and bottom vents. Pile 3 pounds of the charcoal in one half of the cooker, leaving the other half empty. Load a charcoal chimney one-quarter full of charcoal and light it. When the coals in the chimney are glowing, dump them on top of the pile of charcoal already in the cooker. Set half the wood on top of the coals, replace the grate, and put the ribs over the side with no coals (the indirect cooking area), bone side down. Close the lid.

Don't open the cooker for 1 hour, but keep a close eye on the temperature (see page 84 for how best to assess and monitor cooker temperature); when it reaches 230°, which might happen very quickly, close the vents about halfway so that less air comes in to feed the fire and the heat in the cooker rises slowly. Let the temperature climb to between 250° and 275° (see page 77 for how to determine your target temperature). **Maintain your target temperature for the duration of the cook.**

Throughout the entirety of the cook, be on the lookout for fluctuations in cooker temperature; whenever it dips more than 5° and opening the vents isn't sufficient to bring it back up, it's time to add a few hot coals from the chimney. You'll need to prepare another round of charcoal every few hours as needed. If at any point the temperature climbs above your target by more than 5°, close the top and bottom vents further so that even less air comes in to feed the fire.

Continue smoking the ribs for another hour, periodically checking the temperature and color of the meat; rotate as needed to brown evenly. Use an instant-read thermometer to check the temperature of the meat: Insert the probe into a rib, not touching bone. You're looking for a slow and steady climb toward 175°. As the wood burns throughout the cook, continue to add the other pieces until the meat reaches between 135° and 140°.

Continue cooking the ribs, checking internal temperature every 30 minutes or so, until the temperature of the thickest part of a rib reads between 175° and 180°. Take the ribs off the cooker, wrap them in pink butcher paper, and return them to the cooker. (Don't worry, the paper won't catch fire.) Cook the ribs for another hour, or until the internal temperature is between 185° and 190° (you can poke the probe right through the paper). Transfer the wrapped ribs to the cooler, close the lid, and leave the parcel be in the cooler for at least 1 hour and up to 3 hours.

Note: If you don't want to use the wrapping/cooler method, cook the ribs to an internal temperature between 195° and 200°, then set them on a cutting board to rest, uncovered, for 20 to 30 minutes.

To serve, cut the rack into single-bone sections. One bone per person is a generous serving; each individual bone will weigh about 1 pound. Alternatively, slice the meat off the bones and serve in smaller portions.

BEST-EVER BACKYARD BRISKET

MAKES 4 TO 5½ POUNDS MEAT, ENOUGH FOR 16 LARGE SERVINGS OR SANDWICHES, PLUS TRIMMINGS FOR SEASONING OTHER DISHES

If there is one meat that perfectly exemplifies the transformative power of barbecue, it's brisket. When bathed in smoke and cooked ever so slowly over indirect heat, the collagen and intramuscular fibers of this humble, tough, bland piece of meat melt away, mixing and mingling with a salty, peppery rub to create a piece of meat that's magically rich and tender inside, and surrounded with intensely flavored bark.

The brisket cut is made up of two sections: the nose—also known as the deckle or the point—and the flat. The nose is thick and fatty and laced with collagen and connective tissue, while the flat is thin and much leaner, with virtually no fat. Cooking brisket properly—so that both sides are done at the same time and the lean side is moist and juicy—is truly an art. But it's one you can master.

Starting with quality meat is important. We like to cook Certified Angus Beef, prime or choice grade. Prime will have the most marbling throughout, which renders over the course of cooking to create the juiciest piece of meat.

Careful trimming is also essential: The thick outer layer of fat and the large pocket of fat along one side, which form a seam between the point and the flat, are too substantial to render completely, so both of those need to be pared way down, but not removed altogether. We leave about ¼ inch of fat, which, as it renders, merges with the peppery rub, forming a thick, flavorful bark. We also reserve and cook the trimmed fat alongside the meat.

Finishing a brisket by wrapping it in butcher paper and putting in a cooler is nothing new—it's a well-established technique for relaxing the meat. The cooler also serves as a holding cabinet and will keep the brisket warm for several hours if you don't open it—handy for a cook-ahead situation.

What *is* new is the practice of wrapping brisket in pink butcher paper before its final hour on the cooker, and taking the meat to a high temperature in order to create a brisket that's a little softer, so that it jiggles when you poke it. This method was pioneered by next-generation cooking masters in Austin, namely John Lewis and Aaron Franklin. The paper is porous; it protects the meat from air and heat while still allowing steam to escape, so the beautiful bark you worked so hard to create won't get soggy. We also use this technique with beef ribs (page 108).

When it comes to carving, brisket has a jumbled-up internal structure and the grain will suddenly change partway in. Proceed carefully as you're carving, always

cutting against the grain, and shifting your angle when the grain changes direction. Meat cut with the grain will be tough, not tender. A long, sharp carving knife is helpful when working with brisket. We reach for our R. Murphy 10-inch butcher knife or slicing knife and the Victorinox 12-inch Fibrox Pro slicing knife (see page 322).

Leftover brisket can be chopped or cubed and added to baked beans, chili, and—yes, indeed—macaroni and cheese. Brisket loses up to two thirds of its weight during the cooking process, so a 12- to 16-pound brisket will end up being 4 to 5½ pounds of meat, some of which will be fat and scraps that can be saved for seasoning. We stockpile all of the cooked fatty trimmings in the freezer. When we've collected a good amount, we chop it up, sauté it, and use it, instead of bacon, to season green beans and collards (page 220). The combination of rub, smoke, fat, and bits of meat delivers a big punch of flavor.

One 12- to 16-pound whole beef brisket (nose on; prime or choice grade), very cold

Mustard Slather (page 31)

Texas Forever Brisket Rub (page 30)

FOR SANDWICHES

Brioche buns

Pure Magic dry rub (page 29) or your choice

Hog Wash Vinegar Splash (page 40)

Apple City Barbecue Sauce (page 36), Private Reserve Mustard Sauce (page 39), or your choice, warm

Pickled Red Onions (page 49)

Tangy Vinegar Cole Slaw (page 214)

Sliced cooked sausage (optional)

Pulled pork (page 99; optional)

20 pounds good-quality lump charcoal

4 small (8-inch) pieces of post oak or 8 store-bought chunks

Pink butcher paper (see page 76)

25- to 38-quart insulated cooler, large enough to fit the meat with room to spare (not Styrofoam or vinyl—we use Igloo, Rubbermaid, or Yeti; optional)

Prep the meat: Remove and reserve the excess fat from all sides of the brisket and from the deep pocket of fat where the nose and flat are attached, taking care to leave a ¼-inch layer, which is enough to both protect the meat while it's cooking and render into a nice outer bark that you can serve up and enjoy (rather than one that's formed atop an inedible, thick layer of fat that has to be sliced off and discarded). Use your hands to cover the entire brisket with a thin layer of Mustard Slather. Sprinkle the entire brisket with a layer of the dry rub. Do the same on the trimmed fat.

Set up the cooker for indirect-heat smoking: Open the top and bottom vents. Pile 3 pounds of the charcoal in one half of the cooker, leaving the other half empty. Load a charcoal chimney one-quarter full of charcoal and light it. When the coals in the chimney are glowing, dump them on top of the pile of charcoal in the cooker. Set half of the wood on top of the coals, replace the grate, and put the meat, fat side up, and the trimmed fat over the side with no coals (the indirect cooking area). Close the lid.

WHY WAGYU?

For a special treat, cook a Snake River Farms Wagyu brisket, available via mail order (see page 324). Wagyu beef is butchered from Japanese cows whose breeding is carefully planned and tracked. These cows were originally bred for use in heavy work, and their intramuscular system is woven with extra ribbons of fat that provide the animal with a readily available energy source. This makes Wagyu meat exquisitely tender; even the flat is marbled, and the fat renders completely, leaving the meat with a buttery texture. There are different grades of Wagyu, based on the amount of marbling.

Keep a close eye on the temperature (see page 84 for how best to assess and monitor cooker temperature); when it reaches 200°, which might happen very quickly, close the vents about halfway so that less air comes in to feed the fire and the cooker heat rises slowly. Let the temperature climb to between 225° and 250° (see page 77 for how to determine your target temperature). **Maintain your target temperature for the duration of the cook.**

Throughout the entirety of the cook, be on the lookout for fluctuations in cooker temperature; whenever it dips more than 5° and opening the vents isn't sufficient to bring it back up, it's time to add a few hot coals from the chimney. You'll need to prepare another round of charcoal every few hours as needed. If at any point the temperature climbs above your target by more than 5°, close the top and bottom vents further so that even less air comes in to feed the fire.

After the brisket has been on the cooker for 3 hours, periodically check the edges of the meat closest to the fire. Rotate the meat as needed to brown evenly, but never flip it over. Use an instant-read thermometer to check the temperature of the meat: Insert the probe into the thickest part; you're looking for a slow and steady climb toward 175°. As the wood burns throughout the cook, continue to add the other pieces until the meat reaches between 135° and 140°. The meat may get very dark or even blacken, and for brisket that is a good thing. Take the pieces of fat off the pit when they are deep brown and shriveled.

When the temperature in the thickest part of the brisket reaches between 175° and 180° (which could take upward of 12 more hours depending upon weight and cooking temperature), take the brisket off the cooker, wrap it in pink butcher paper, and return it to the cooker. (Don't worry, the paper won't catch fire.) Cook the brisket until the internal temperature is 185° to 190° (you can poke the probe right through the paper). Transfer the wrapped brisket from the cooker

to the cooler, close the lid, and leave it be in the cooler for at least 1 hour and up to 3 hours.

Note: If you don't want to use the wrapping/cooler method, cook the brisket to an internal temperature between 185° and 190°, then set it on a cutting board to rest, uncovered, for 20 to 30 minutes.

Brisket should be cut against the grain; slice off one corner of the flat to check the direction of the grain. Slice the flat in ¼-inch slices; the point, with its fattier composition, needs to be sliced a little thicker. Serve sliced on its own, or in sandwiches, which can be made with slices of lean brisket only, or with a chopped mix of fatty point and lean flat pieces. (See page 116 for directions on using the nose to make Burnt Ends.) Wrap the fat trimmings and other scraps in plastic wrap, put it in a freezer bag, and keep in the freezer to use for seasoning collards (page 220) and such.

For sandwiches: Pile sliced or chopped brisket on the bottom of each bun, sprinkle with dry rub, add a splash of Hog Wash and layer on barbecue sauce, if you like, then top with Pickled Red Onions and/or Tangy Vinegar Cole Slaw.

To make a Texas-style sandwich, add a layer of sliced sausage and some pulled pork as well (see photo, page 114).

COMPETITION BRISKET

On the competition circuit, "brisket" has the texture and flavor of pot roast. That is not what we're teaching you to make here, and it's not what you are served in a good barbecue restaurant.

For competitions, the meat is injected with beef broth, then wrapped up and simmered in broth to infuse it with flavor and make it extra tender. Why? Because it's one-bite brisket—as in, the judges evaluate it on the basis of a single bite that's all about tenderness and a super intense flavor. So the bark and all of the other delicious nuances of a true barbecue brisket are of no consequence.

Now, we like pot roast just fine. We also like winning, so if we're cooking in a competition, we're gonna make brisket that way, too, because that's the expectation and that's what takes the prize. But at home and at 17th Street, our brisket tastes like brisket in all its natural glory.

BURNT ENDS

MAKES 20 TO 25 PIECES

Back in the day, "burnt ends" was the name for the flavorful bits of rub- and smoke-laden bark and meat that fell off brisket when it was being sliced. At the legendary Arthur Bryant's Barbeque, in Kansas City, the guys slicing the brisket sometimes handed tidbits of burnt ends to guests passing their way along the ordering counter. Now burnt ends are a specialty unto themselves.

Now that they are a popular menu item, burnt ends are made from the point end of the brisket—the fatty cut that is laced with delicate strands of collagen and connective tissue and therefore needs to be fully rendered to be done. To make burnt ends, instead of serving the point along with the rest of the cooked brisket, you separate it from the flat, cut it into 1- to 1½-inch cubes, re-season it, and put it back on the cooker for another hour or so to absorb more spice and sauce and develop an all-over crusty bark. The result is a chewy, ultra savory bite of beef.

Point portion of a cooked 10- to 12-pound brisket (page 110)

2 tablespoons to ¼ cup Pure Magic dry rub (page 29) or your choice

1 cup Apple City Barbecue Sauce (page 36) or your choice

3 to 5 pounds good-quality lump charcoal

Heavy-duty aluminum foil, punched with a few holes, or a rimmed baking sheet fitted with a wire rack

Cut the meat into 1- to 1½-inch cubes, put it in a large bowl, and toss with enough of dry rub to coat evenly. Pour in the sauce and toss again, coating liberally.

Keep the fire from the brisket cook going, adding more hot coals and maintaining your target temperature between 250° and 275°.

Transfer the meat to the foil and put it on the cooker. Close the lid.

Prepare another round of charcoal in the chimney, filling it halfway and lighting it. If the cooker temperature dips more than 5° below your target and adjusting the vents doesn't bring it back up, add a few more coals. If the cooker temperature climbs more than 5° above your target, close the vents further to allow even less air to feed the fire.

Cook the meat until the sauce is set, forming a bark all over each piece, 1 to 1½ hours.

Serve the burnt ends on a tray with toothpicks or use them to make sandwiches.

PASTRAMI ON THE PIT

MAKES 4 TO 5½ POUNDS MEAT, ENOUGH FOR 16 LARGE SERVINGS OR SANDWICHES, PLUS TRIMMINGS TO USE FOR SEASONING OTHER DISHES

Pastrami is brisket that's been cured in a brine and smoked, with or without a peppery dry rub. Curing the meat deeply seasons it with salt, sugar, and aromatic spices, giving it a distinct flavor, a tender texture, and a deep red or purplish hue. (Corned beef is yet another preparation of the same brisket cut—brined and then boiled rather than smoked, and flavored only by the spices in the brine.)

The critical factors in making good pastrami, aside from flavorful brine and rub, are patience and refrigerator space. Make the brine a day in advance so it has time to thoroughly steep and chill. After that, the meat needs to soak in the brine, undisturbed, for 8 to 10 days. You'll need a 5-gallon brining bucket or a food-grade plastic storage container large enough to accommodate both the meat and enough brine to cover it by an inch or so. You may need to take a shelf out of your refrigerator to make room. Duration is also crucial; if the meat isn't brined long enough, it won't take on that full pastrami flavor. Note that the process takes ten-plus days: one day for the brine to chill, at least eight days for the meat to soak, and a full day for the cook.

Another important factor is fat. Chilled fat is easier to trim, so keep the brisket refrigerated until you're ready to prep it, and when trimming the meat, take care to leave a ⅛- to ¼-inch layer, which is enough to both protect the meat while it's cooking and render into a nice outer bark you can serve up and enjoy (rather than one that's formed atop an inedible, thick layer of fat that has to be sliced off and discarded). Reserve the excess fat from all sides of the meat.

Our favorite way to serve pastrami is to slice it thinly and make a traditional Reuben sandwich: topped with sauerkraut, Swiss cheese, and Russian dressing, and griddled on buttered marbled rye so the cheese melts and mingles with the kraut.

You can also use this brine to cure pork belly (see page 154), bacon, beef ribs, duck, or most any other cut of meat. Brining time will vary based on the cut of meat.

BRINE

2 cups 17th Street Sugar Cure (see Resources, page 321)

2 cups white vinegar

¼ cup sugar

12 garlic cloves, coarsely chopped

8 bay leaves, crumbled

½ cup pickling spice

One 12- to 16-pound whole brisket (nose on; prime or choice), very cold

Mustard Slather (page 31)

Texas Forever Brisket Rub (page 30)

Large stainless-steel stockpot

Food-grade brining bucket or plastic container large enough to fit the brisket submerged in brine (see page 75)

A plate and a weight to help hold the brisket down in case it floats to the top (it must be submerged; a large rock or brick works well)

20 pounds good-quality lump charcoal

4 small (8-inch) pieces of apple wood or 8 store-bought chunks

Pink butcher paper (see page 76)

25- to 38-quart insulated cooler, large enough to fit the meat with room to spare (not Styrofoam or vinyl—we use Igloo, Rubbermaid, or Yeti)

Make room in your refrigerator to fit the large container in which you'll be brining the pastrami.

Prepare the brine one day in advance: Combine 2 gallons water, the cure, vinegar, sugar, garlic, bay leaves, and pickling spice in a stockpot and stir to mix. Bring to a boil, simmer for 30 minutes until it's the color of tea, and then take the pot off the heat. Cool to room temperature, then chill in the refrigerator overnight.

While the brine is chilling, take the brisket out of the refrigerator and trim the visible fat on all sides of the meat to a ⅛- to ¼-inch layer. Using a two-pronged meat fork, poke holes all over the brisket. Reserve the trimmed fat.

Put the meat and the fat trimmings in the bucket and pour the chilled brine over the top, covering by at least 1 inch. Set a plate and a weight on top of the brisket to keep it submerged. Cover the container with a lid or plastic wrap, transfer to the refrigerator, and do not disturb for at least 8 and up to 10 days.

Remove the meat and the trimmings from the brine and discard the liquid and seasonings. Pat the excess moisture from the meat with paper towels. Use your hands to cover the entire brisket with a thin layer of Mustard Slather. Sprinkle the entire brisket with a layer of the dry rub.

Cook, rest, and slice as instructed for brisket (pages 110 to 115).

Wrap the fat trimmings and other scraps in plastic wrap, put it in a freezer bag, and keep in the freezer to use for seasoning collards (page 220) and such.

(continued)

↓

REUBEN SANDWICH

MAKES 1 SANDWICH

Buttermilk Russian
(page 61)

2 pieces marble rye bread

2 to 3 tablespoons
unsalted butter

Good-quality jarred
sauerkraut, drained

Sliced Swiss cheese

Spread a thin layer of Buttermilk Russian on one side of each slice of bread. Melt the butter in a skillet and lay the bread slices in the skillet, sauced side up, to brown. Add a few tablespoons of sauerkraut to the skillet to warm, then add the pastrami to the skillet, just long enough to slightly warm it. Add a slice of cheese to one piece of the bread. When the cheese starts to melt, layer the pastrami on top, followed by the sauerkraut and the other slice of bread. Cut the sandwich in half and serve.

SHOE SHOPPING WITH JEFFREY STEINGARTEN

When our first book, *Peace, Love, and Barbecue,* was nominated for a James Beard award, we traveled to New York City for the ceremony. Jeffrey Steingarten, one of the world's most acclaimed food writers and the food critic for *Vogue* magazine, insisted we save room in our schedule for a pastrami sandwich lunch with him at the famous Katz's Delicatessen. Once we were there, Jeffrey led us through the ordering procedure at the hallowed counter as we talked about the nuances of pastrami and corned beef, and devoured the thick, delicious sandwiches. When I mentioned that I needed a pair of shoes to wear that evening, talk turned to Jeffrey's other specialty: fashion. He placed a call to one of his editor friends at *Vogue,* asking where to shop. As luck would have it, we were directed to a street behind Katz's known for a great selection of designer shoes I could have at a (very slight) editorial discount. Jeffrey reeled off names like Manolo and Jimmy Choo as Mike eyed him warily.

The two men set up shop outside, smoking Marlboro Reds, as I tried on dozens of pairs, sticking my foot out the door for opinions. Finally I found the perfect pair of strappy heels. "Yes," Jeffrey nodded. "*Those.*" Mike winced as he pulled from his pocket a wad of money held together with a rubber band and peeled off a few large bills.

My daddy is never going to appreciate fashion, but the man certainly knows his pastrami. At any given time, we have a batch of briskets marinating in our signature brine in the walk-in cooler.

=Amy=

GARLIC-BUTTERED RIBEYE STEAKS

MAKES 4 TO 6 SERVINGS

The term "reverse-sear" refers to flipping the traditional sequence of steak-cooking steps so that the meat is first infused with smoke and searing happens just before serving. This is an easy route to a tender piece of meat with a delicious savory crust, especially if a perfect medium-rare is your goal—which is one of the factors determining a win, according to Steak Cookoff Association guidelines.

We like to cook boneless Certified Angus Beef prime or choice grade meat. Bone-in or boneless—the choice is yours.

4 to 6 ribeye steaks (about 1 pound each, 1 to 1½ inches thick, prime or choice)

Steakhouse Shake (page 32) or kosher salt and pepper

Herb and Garlic Butter (page 238), chilled, for serving

¼ cup crumbled blue cheese, for serving (optional)

2 pounds good-quality lump charcoal

1 small (8-inch) piece of apple wood or 2 store-bought chunks

Up to 40 minutes prior to cooking, season the steak generously with the shake. Set the steaks on a baking sheet and refrigerate them, loosely covered, until you're ready to grill.

Set up the cooker for indirect-heat smoking: Open the top and bottom vents. Load a charcoal chimney one-quarter full of charcoal and light it. When the coals in the chimney are glowing, dump them on one side of the cooker. Set the wood on top of the coals, replace the grate, and put the steaks over the side with no coals (the indirect cooking area). Close the lid.

Don't open the cooker for 15 minutes, but keep a close eye on the temperature (see page 84 for how best to assess and monitor cooker temperature); when it reaches 200°, which might happen very quickly, close the vents about halfway so that less air comes in to feed the fire and the heat in the cooker rises slowly. Let the temperature climb to between 225° and 250° (see page 77 for how to determine your target temperature). **Maintain your target temperature;** if at any point it climbs more than 5° above your target, close the top and bottom vents further so that even less air comes in to feed the fire.

(continued)

↓

After 15 minutes, open the lid of the cooker and use an instant-read thermometer to check the internal temperature of the thickest part of the steak; you are looking for a slow and steady climb to 105° (for rare) or 110° (for medium-rare). This will take no longer than 20 minutes.

After you check the meat temperature, reload the chimney halfway with charcoal and light it. You'll soon need these additional hot coals to sear the steaks at the finishing stage, after they're done smoking.

When the steaks are 105° for rare or 110° for medium-rare, set them aside on a baking sheet. Working quickly, add the hot coals and spread them out all over the bottom of the cooker. Replace the grate and put the steaks directly over the hot coals. Sear for a minute or two on each side, just until a brown crust forms and the internal temperature is 120° for rare or 130° for medium-rare. Top each steak with a slice of Herb and Garlic Butter, and blue cheese if you like, and serve.

BIRD ON A FIRE

MAKES 2 TO 4 SERVINGS

When it's done right, smoked chicken is juicy and lusciously redolent of smoke, spice, and sauce, along with the flavor of the meat itself—all in equal measure. We lightly season the outside of the bird with garlic salt to draw moisture from the skin so the fat renders and the skin comes out deliciously crispy.

Half-birds are easier to position and move around than whole ones. And the advantages of half-chickens over separated chicken parts include that you have fewer pieces to corral, less juice draining from the meat while it cooks, and you end up with larger expanses of crispy skin. Use apple, wild cherry, peach, or pecan woods for chicken; hard woods such as hickory or oak impart an overpoweringly strong flavor.

There is no end to the delicious uses for leftover smoky chicken—shredded, cubed, or sliced. Our favorite ways to repurpose include atop salads, baked potatoes, and nachos.

1 whole chicken (3 to 3½ pounds), very cold	3 to 5 pounds good-quality lump charcoal	String mop (see page 76)
Garlic salt	1 small (8-inch) piece of apple wood or 2 store-bought chunks	
Dry rub (your choice)		
Barbecue sauce (your choice), warm		

Use poultry shears to cut along each side of the backbone to remove it; discard. Open up the bird, lay it skin side up on a cutting board, and press down firmly to flatten. Trim off and discard the hunk of excess fat at the tail end and cut through the breastbone to halve the chicken. Flip the halves over and straighten out the skin on each half. Twist each wing tip upward and over the rest of the wing and tuck it in so that the "elbow" of the wing sticks up in the air. (This is purely for aesthetics; if you leave the wing be, there will be a white spot where the smoke doesn't hit the skin.)

Very lightly season the chicken with garlic salt and dry rub, coating so thinly that it's barely visible. Set the chicken halves on a baking sheet, cover them with plastic wrap, and refrigerate until you're ready to put them on the cooker.

Set up the cooker for indirect-heat smoking: Open the top and bottom vents. Pile 3 pounds of the charcoal in one half of the cooker, leaving the other half empty. Load a chimney no more than one-quarter full of charcoal and light it.

(continued)
↓

When the coals are glowing, dump them on top of the pile of charcoal in the cooker. Set the wood on top of the coals, replace the grate, and put the chicken on, bone side down, over the side with no coals (the indirect cooking area). Close the lid.

Don't open the cooker for 1 hour, but keep a close eye on the temperature (see page 84 for how best to assess and monitor cooker temperature); when it reaches 185°, which might happen very quickly, close the vents about halfway so that less air comes in to feed the fire and the heat in the cooker rises slowly. Let the temperature climb to between 250° and 275° (see page 77 for how to determine your target temperature). **Maintain your target temperature for the duration of the cook.**

Throughout the entirety of the cook, be on the lookout for fluctuations in cooker temperature. If it dips more than 5° below your target and opening the vents isn't sufficient to bring it back up, you will need to add a few coals. If at any point the temperature climbs above your target by more than 5°, close the top and bottom vents further so that even less air comes in to feed the fire.

After an hour, open the lid and check the edges of the chicken closest to the fire. If they look like they're beginning to brown, rotate the chicken, moving the half farther away from the fire and placing it closer, and vice versa.

Close the lid and continue smoking the chicken for another hour, checking the color and the edges every 20 minutes. Never flip the pieces over; instead, continue rotating them to cook evenly.

Prepare another round of charcoal in the chimney as needed. This cook should not require more charcoal than the initial amount, but we always keep some coals at the ready just in case more are needed to maintain target cooker temperature.

After the chicken has been on the cooker for 2 hours, use an instant-read thermometer to check for doneness: Insert the probe into the thickest part of the thigh; if the probe slides in easily, the meat is nearly done. The temperature will read between 165° and 170°.

When the temperature reaches 170°, mop the chicken with a thin coat of sauce (it will ball up a bit—don't worry), then close the lid for just a minute to let it dry a bit. Mop with a second thin coat and give a final sprinkle of dry rub. Pull the chicken halves off the cooker and set them on a cutting board to rest, uncovered, for about 10 minutes before serving.

(OPPOSITE) Half chickens hanging in a Pit Barrel Cooker

BIRD BRINE

When you brine poultry, depending on the type of brine and the length of the soak, the brine typically penetrates ⅛ to ¼ inch, really just flavoring the outside. You can taste that, though, because the flavor will hit your tongue as soon as you bite into it. We happen to like the flavor of chicken and turkey with no brine. So that's how we smoke 'em.

PURE MAGIC TURKEY BREAST

MAKES ABOUT 6 POUNDS

Even though it has virtually no fat, turkey breast can be cooked to moist, flavorful perfection if you maintain a low, consistent temperature and don't overcook. Buy all-natural turkey, which means reading ingredient labels carefully and steering clear of anything with additives: Almost all turkey out there has been injected with a saline solution or stuff that's supposed to taste like butter. Use apple, wild cherry, peach, or pecan wood; the smoke flavor from hard woods such as hickory or oak will impart too strong a flavor.

Smoking a boneless breast rather than a whole bird means zero waste, as well as a relatively short cook—about 3 hours. When we cook turkey at home, we take it off the cooker between 155° and 160°, whereas cooking charts list the USDA/CDC–sanctioned 165°.

Turkey has the best flavor and is easiest to slice when it's chilled, and that's how we always serve it, whether it's as a sandwich or a meat plate. Slice thinly for sandwiches, thicker to serve on its own.

Leftover smoked turkey is at least as versatile as chicken. One of our favorite ways to repurpose it is to julienne the small ends of the breast and pile atop a chef's salad.

Note: In the following recipe, the turkey breast is cooked without the skin, which means the applied seasonings will impart flavor to the meat. You could also opt to cook the two breast halves skin on, which creates a good protective barrier for keeping the meat moist, but the skin will be rubbery, oily, and inedible, and any seasoning applied won't penetrate the skin to flavor the meat. However, when the turkey breast is done, you can remove the skin, lightly coat it with additional dry rub, and grill it directly over the coals until it's browned and sizzling, and enjoy pieces of crispy, flavor-packed turkey skin.

1 whole turkey breast (7 to 8 pounds), very cold	Pure Magic dry rub (page 29) or your choice	4 to 5 pounds good-quality lump charcoal (we use Royal Oak)
Mustard Slather (page 31)		1 small (8-inch) piece of apple wood or 2 store-bought chunks

Remove the skin from the turkey breast. Using a flexible boning knife and following the visible fat line between the skin and the top of the meat as a guide, split the two lobes off the bone. Discard the bones and skin. Brush the meat with the thinnest possible coat of Mustard Slather, just enough to help the rub adhere. Sprinkle all over with a very light coat of dry rub. Set the turkey breast halves on a baking sheet, cover them with plastic wrap, and refrigerate until you're ready to put them on the cooker.

Set up the cooker for indirect-heat smoking: Open the top and bottom vents. Pile 3 pounds of the charcoal in one half of the cooker, leaving the other half empty. Load a charcoal chimney one-quarter full of charcoal and light it. When the coals in the chimney are glowing, dump them on top of the pile of charcoal already in the cooker. Set the wood on top of the coals, replace the grate, and put the turkey breast halves on, flatter side down, over the side with no coals (the indirect cooking area).

Don't open the lid for 1 hour but keep a close eye on the temperature (see page 84 for how best to assess and monitor cooker temperature); when it reaches 185°, which might happen very quickly, close the vents about halfway so that less air comes in to feed the fire and the heat in the cooker rises more slowly. Let the temperature climb to about 225° (see page 77 for how to determine your target temperature). **Maintain your target temperature for the duration of the cook.**

Throughout the entirety of the cook, be on the lookout for fluctuations in cooker temperature. If it dips more than 5° below your target and opening the vents isn't sufficient to bring it back up, you will need to add a few coals. If at any point the temperature climbs above your target by more than 5°, close the top and bottom vents further so that even less air comes in to feed the fire.

After an hour, open the lid and check the edges of the turkey closest to the fire. If they look like they're beginning to brown, rotate the turkey, moving the half that is farther away from the fire closer, and vice versa.

Close the lid and continue smoking the turkey for another hour, checking the color and the edges every 20 minutes. Never flip the pieces over; instead, continue rotating them to cook evenly.

Prepare another round of charcoal as needed. This cook may not require more charcoal than the initial amount, but we always keep some coals at the ready just in case more are needed to maintain the temperature.

After the turkey has been on the cooker for 2 hours, use an instant-read thermometer to check for doneness: Insert the probe into the thickest part of the breast; if the probe slides in easily, the meat is nearly done. The temperature should read between 155° and 160°.

When the temperature reaches 160°, take the turkey off the cooker and set it on a cutting board or baking sheet to rest, tented with foil, for 25 to 30 minutes. The temperature inside the breast will continue to rise, gaining the necessary 5°.

Chill the turkey before slicing about ⅛ inch thick across the grain.

BARBECUE PARFAITS

MAKES 8 PARFAITS

Parfaits are a perfect way to utilize leftover meat and side dishes from a barbecue. Colorful and appealing, these are perfect as an entire meal; make miniatures for a party.

2 cups corn chips, Fritos, or tortilla chips

2 cups Mike's From-Scratch Baked Beans (page 224)

2 cups pulled pork (One-Seven Heaven Pork Shoulder, page 96) or chopped Best-Ever Backyard Brisket (page 110), Bird on a Fire (page 125), or Pure Magic Turkey Breast (page 129)

2 cups Tangy Vinegar Cole Slaw (page 214)

Barbecue sauce (your choice)

Dry rub (your choice)

8 mason jars or Weck jars (8- to 12-ounce capacity)

Put ¼ cup corn chips in the bottom of each jar. Top with ¼ cup baked beans, then ¼ cup pork, beef, chicken, or turkey. Add ¼ cup cole slaw on top of the meat. Adjust these measurements based on the size of your jar. Drizzle with barbecue sauce and sprinkle with dry rub.

HOUSE-GROUND BEER BRATS

MAKES ABOUT 30 (6-INCH) SAUSAGES, 6 TO SERVE AND 24 TO FREEZE

Sausage is the next big thing in barbecue. The possibilities for meat and seasoning combinations are endless, and making sausage is an excellent way to use scraps of meat that might otherwise be discarded. Once you get the hang of grinding the meat and stuffing the casing, the process is fun. It's easiest to use presoaked casing, available from butcher shops. You can quickly make a pile of sausages, some to eat now and dozens more to stock your freezer.

This classic bratwurst is a blend of ground pork meat with curing salt and aromatic spices. The sausage is poached in dark beer before being browned all over in a cast-iron skillet with peppers and onions.

Sausage casings, preferably presoaked (see Resources, page 321)

9 pounds pork, from butt or shoulder, very cold, cut into 4-x-2-inch chunks or ground by the butcher

1½ cups powdered whole milk

5½ tablespoons coarsely ground black pepper

4½ tablespoons kosher salt

3 tablespoons granulated garlic

2 tablespoons ground fennel seed

1 tablespoon sweet Hungarian paprika

1 tablespoon ground white pepper

1 tablespoon ground nutmeg

1½ teaspoons pink curing salt

FOR SERVING

Four 12-ounce bottles or cans dark beer

2 tablespoons lard or olive oil

1 sweet onion, sliced

1 red pepper, sliced

1 green pepper, sliced

6 hot dog buns or Italian sandwich rolls (optional)

Meat grinder (see page 76) fitted with a ⅜-inch grinding plate

Sausage stuffer (see Resources, page 321)

8-inch square disposable aluminum baking pan

3 pounds good-quality lump charcoal

1 small (8-inch) piece of apple wood or 2 store-bought chunks

12-inch cast-iron skillet

If the casings are not presoaked, rinse them under cool running water, then soak in a bowl of cool water for about 30 minutes to render out some of the brine and make the casings pliable. Discard the soaking water and refill the bowl with warm water; keep the casings in the warm water while you are making the sausage.

Grind the pork into a very cold large bowl. In a medium bowl, combine the powdered milk and other dry ingredients and whisk to blend. Add the spice

mixture to the ground meat and use your hands to thoroughly mix until well combined. Cover the bowl and refrigerate until you are ready to stuff the sausage.

Thread the sausage stuffer funnel with an entire length of casing. Position a baking sheet underneath the stuffer to catch the sausage and lightly sprinkle water over the surface of the baking sheet so the filled sausage casing won't stick. Pull 2 inches of the casing out and twist it firmly to secure the end. Load ground meat into the stuffer. Using even pressure, begin filling the casing, trying to keep the diameter of the sausage consistent. Twist the casing every 6 inches to create 6 links; twist enough to create about an inch of twisted casing. After you've filled about 3 feet, examine the coil of sausage for air pockets and prick them with a toothpick to puncture the casing and release the air. Snip in the middle of each twist to separate the links; the ends will self-seal and stay twisted. Repeat the process to make about 24 more sausage links.

Put 6 sausages on a plate and refrigerate until you're ready to cook. Line two baking sheets with parchment paper. Arrange as many sausages as can fit without touching on each sheet and slide one into the freezer. Cover the other with plastic wrap and refrigerate. Once the first round of sausages has frozen solid, transfer them to a freezer bag; squeeze out the air before sealing and return to the freezer. Repeat with the rest of the sausages. Store in the freezer for up to 2 months. (Thaw before cooking.)

If poaching the sausages on the cooker, set up the cooker for direct cooking: Open the top and bottom vents. Pile 2 pounds of the charcoal in the bottom. Load a charcoal chimney one-quarter full of charcoal and light it. When the coals in the chimney are glowing, dump them on top of the pile of charcoal in the cooker. Set the wood on top of the coals in the cooker and replace the grate. Close the lid and adjust the vents as necessary to establish a steady temperature between 220° and 230° (see pages 84 and 77 for how best to assess and monitor cooker temperature, and how to determine your target temperature).

Put the 6 sausages on the plate in the disposable pan and pour in enough beer to cover. Set the pan directly over the glowing coals, bring the liquid to a simmer, and continue cooking for 15 minutes. Take the pan off the cooker and transfer the sausages to a baking sheet. (Or, poach the sausages on the stovetop, following the same procedure using a saucepan over medium-high heat.)

Finish the sausages: Melt the lard or heat the oil in the cast-iron skillet on the cooker at 220° to 230° (or on the stovetop over medium-high heat). Add the onions and the red and green peppers and cook for 5 minutes, stirring often to prevent scorching. Add the drained bratwurst and continue cooking, stirring the vegetables often and turning the sausages frequently so the casings don't burst, until the vegetables are softened and the sausages are browned. Alternatively, grill the bratwurst over medium coals until browned, turning frequently so the casings don't burst, and sauté the onions and peppers in a cast-iron pan.

Serve as is, or make sandwiches by putting each bratwurst on a bun along with some onions and peppers.

A HEAVENLY PATTY

Creating a backyard version of a simple but perfect restaurant burger begins, of course, with the meat, ideally a home-ground combination of superior-quality (prime or choice grade Certified Angus Beef) large-muscle meats (no trimmings!), plus just the right amount of fat. Our signature formula is 46 percent brisket, 46 percent chuck (each of which have quite a bit of natural fat), and 8 percent beef fat (ask your butcher for help with the fat). That may seem like a lot of fat, but it's essential for flavor, moisture, and texture. It also serves to hold the burger together; too lean a mix, and the burger will tend to crumble while you're cooking it and will feel like gravel in your mouth. The right amount allows you to serve up a burger that has been cooked all the way to a safe temperature but is still juicy and flavorful.

It is essential to keep the meat very cold before, during, and after grinding—for ease, best texture, and safety. Use a #10 to #12 grinding plate with a ⅜-inch hole size. (A grinder will also set you up to make your own sausage, page 76.) If you don't want to grind the meat yourself, you can have the meat ground to order when you purchase it.

Take care not to overwork the ground meat; you want the texture to remain coarse, and if you knead it you'll end up with mush. Do not mix anything—not even salt—into the meat; instead, season the outside of the burger just before you put it on the grill.

It's also essential to use a light touch when forming the patties. Here's how we do it: Take about ⅓ pound meat and make a loose ball. Play catch with it, tossing it from hand to hand four or five times. This condenses the meat a bit but doesn't put so much pressure on it that it cooks up like a hockey puck. You want tiny air pockets within, where the juices can collect; this will help the meat hold together while you're cooking it. Now press the ball lightly to flatten it to about ½ inch thick. Keeping the patties thin helps you take them to a safe temperature without drying them out. (You can always stack 'em for a thick burger effect).

Lastly, flip your burgers once and only once; repeated turning will wring them dry. Don't press on them with the spatula, and do take them all the way to that 155° internal temperature—the juices will pool on the tops of the burgers and they will be clear, not tinged with pink.

PIMENTO CHEESEBURGERS

MAKES ABOUT 30 PATTIES, 6 TO SERVE AND 24 TO FREEZE

The building that is now 17th Street Barbecue started out as Ellis Tavern in 1925, and it's had multiple names and owners over the years. While these establishments were all bars catering mostly to men, the single constant, as far back as Mike—or anyone in town, for that matter—can remember is that each served two bar snacks: a barbecue sandwich and a hamburger. To this day, our menu still features a quarter-pound burger simply dressed with mustard, onion, and pickle. We think The Original, as we call it, is at its best when spread thickly with pimento cheese, which is house-made in keeping with the Mills family recipe. The rich flavor and creamy texture of the melting pimento cheese take a straightforward, well-executed burger over the top.

This recipe makes a lot of patties so that you can freeze the extra and cook 'em up for truly great backyard burgers any time. Feel free to have the butcher grind the meat together for you when you purchase it.

4 pounds brisket, prime or choice, very cold, cut into 4-x-2-inch chunks

4 pounds chuck, prime or choice, very cold, cut into 4-x-2-inch chunks

1½ pounds beef fat, very cold, cut into 4-x-2-inch chunks

Texas Forever Brisket Rub (page 30) or kosher salt and coarsely ground black pepper

6 hamburger buns

½ to ¾ cup Piquant Pimento Cheese (page 53), slightly softened

Sliced onions, tomatoes, pickles, and other toppings of your choice

Meat grinder (see page 76) fitted with a ⅜-inch grinding plate

3 pounds good-quality lump charcoal

Kitchen scale (optional)

Before grinding, toss the chunks of meat and fat together. Grind the beef into a very cold large bowl. Use your hands to lightly fluff the ground mixture just enough to blend the components; do not overwork. Cover the bowl and refrigerate until you are ready to form the burgers.

Lightly form 6 patties, each about ⅓ pound and ½ inch thick, being careful not to pack or overwork the meat (see page 137). Set the patties on a plate or baking sheet and refrigerate them, loosely covered, until you're ready to grill.

Form 24 more patties. Line two baking sheets with parchment paper. Arrange as many burgers as can fit without touching on one baking sheet and slide the sheet

into the freezer. Put the remaining patties on the other sheet, cover with plastic wrap, and put it in the refrigerator. Once the first round of patties has frozen solid, which can take 2 to 3 hours, layer them with squares of waxed paper, transfer them to a freezer bag, press out all the air before sealing, and put them back in the freezer. Repeat the process in as many batches as needed to freeze the rest of the patties. Store in the freezer for up to 2 months. Thaw in the refrigerator before grilling.

Set up the cooker for direct cooking: Open the top and bottom vents. Pile 2 pounds of the charcoal in the bottom. Load a charcoal chimney one-quarter full of charcoal and light it. When the coals in the chimney are glowing, dump them on top of the pile of charcoal already in the cooker and close the lid. Adjust the vents as necessary to establish a steady temperature between 400° and 450° for direct grilling (see pages 84 and 77 for how best to assess and monitor cooker temperature, and how to determine your target temperature).

Season the burgers one by one as you put them on the cooker: Hold a patty in one hand and generously sprinkle the top with dry rub, then set the patty seasoned side down on the cooker. Press your thumb in the middle of the patty to make a deep indentation. Season the top. Close the lid. Wait for about 5 minutes, then open the lid. Moisture should have pooled on the tops of the patties and the sides should be beginning to sizzle; if this isn't happening yet, close the lid again for 1 more minute.

Flip the burgers and cook for 4 to 5 minutes more, until the internal temperature reaches 155°.

If you prefer toasted buns, about 2 minutes after you've flipped the burgers, put the buns cut side down along the outer edge of the cooker. Watch carefully to make sure they don't burn; toasting them should only take about 1 minute. As soon as the edges begin to brown, use tongs to pull the buns off the cooker and set on a platter.

Just before pulling the burgers off the cooker, top each with a heaping tablespoon of pimento cheese. Use a spatula to transfer the hamburgers to the bottom buns. If you prefer larger burgers, use 2 patties, topping each with a dollop of pimento cheese. Top as desired and serve.

SAFETY NOTE

In order to prevent the risk of *E. coli* infection, the internal temperature of your burgers needs to reach 155° and stay there for at least 20 seconds.

POTBELLY PORK BURGERS

MAKES ABOUT 30 PATTIES, 6 TO SERVE AND 24 TO FREEZE

Pleasingly porky and juicy, with a milder flavor than a hamburger, a grilled pork burger is a great alternative to beef. What began as our way to use unevenly cut pork steaks has become a favorite both as a menu item at 17th Street and at our family cookouts. As with hamburgers, it is crucial to use good-quality, whole cuts of meat (no trimmings!), and the meat-to-fat ratio is important. The natural fat and marbling in pork shoulder is just the right amount. If you don't want to grind the meat yourself, you can have the meat ground to order when you purchase it.

This recipe makes a bulk amount of burgers, so that you can have them on hand to enjoy anytime.

9 pounds boneless pork shoulder, very cold, cut into 4-x-2-inch chunks or ground by the butcher

Steakhouse Shake (page 32) or kosher salt and freshly ground black pepper

6 hamburger buns

Sliced cheese, onions, tomatoes, pickles, and other toppings of your choice

Meat grinder (see page 76) fitted with a ⅜-inch grinding plate

3 pounds good-quality lump charcoal

Grind the pork into a very cold large bowl. Use your hands to lightly fluff the ground meat just enough to distribute any pockets of fat; do not overwork. Cover the bowl and refrigerate until you are ready form the patties.

Lightly form 6 patties, each about ⅓ pound and ½ inch thick, being careful not to pack or overwork the meat (see page 137). Set the patties on a plate and refrigerate them, loosely covered, until you're ready to grill.

Form about 24 more patties. Line two baking sheets with parchment paper. Arrange as many patties as can fit without touching on one baking sheet and slide the sheet into the freezer. Put the remaining patties on the other sheet, cover with plastic wrap, and put it in the refrigerator. Once the first round of patties has frozen solid, which can take 2 to 3 hours, layer them with squares of waxed paper, transfer them to a freezer bag, press out all the air before sealing, and put them back in the freezer. Repeat the process in as many batches as needed to freeze the rest of the patties. Store in the freezer for up to 2 months. Thaw in the refrigerator before grilling.

(continued)

↓

Set up the cooker for direct cooking: Open the top and bottom vents. Pile 2 pounds of the charcoal in the bottom. Load a charcoal chimney one-quarter full of charcoal and light it. When the coals in the chimney are glowing, dump them on top of the pile of charcoal already in the cooker and close the lid. Adjust the vents as necessary to establish a steady temperature between 400° and 450° for direct grilling (see pages 84 and 77 for how best to assess and monitor cooker temperature, and how to determine your target temperature).

Season the patties one by one as you put them on the cooker: Hold each patty in one hand and generously sprinkle the top with shake, then set the patty, seasoned side down, on the cooker. Press your thumb into the middle of each patty to make a deep indentation. Season the tops and close the lid. Wait for about 5 minutes, then open the lid. Moisture should have pooled on the tops of the patties, and the sides should be beginning to sizzle; if this isn't happening yet, close the lid again for 1 minute more.

Flip the burgers and cook for 4 to 5 minutes more, until the internal temperature reaches 160°.

If you prefer toasted buns, about 2 minutes after you've flipped the burgers, put the buns, cut side down, along the outer edge of the cooker. Watch carefully to make sure they don't burn; toasting them should only take about 1 minute. As soon as the edges begin to brown, use tongs to pull the buns off the cooker and set them on a platter.

Use a spatula to transfer the patties to the bottom buns. Top as desired and serve.

Modern-day resurrection: Skyline Grocery, in its heyday. This building is now The Warehouse at I7th Street.

ORGSMILLER AND SONS
LESALE GROCERS
HENRY BORGSMILLER SONS
Skyline
HENRY BORGSMILLER SONS
Skyline
HENRY BORGSMILLER SONS
MURPHYSBORO ILL.
Skyline
Phone 304
4

HYMN TO OUR HOMETOWN, SUNG IN TWO PARTS

The Murphysboro of my childhood was a mecca, abuzz with activity, especially on the weekends when farmers and other folks from outlying areas came into town to shop. It was the 1940s and '50s, and the population was close to what it is now (just shy of 8,000 at last count), but there was a whole lot more commerce going on.

The downtown area where our restaurant stands today was a bustling business and industrial district. Murphysboro was a stop on two major railroads serving the central United States—the Illinois Central and the GM&O—and trains trundled through, day and night, loading and unloading passengers as well as a steady flow of raw materials and finished goods going to and from the various factories in town. Those trains were also the means whereby our region exported huge quantities of agricultural crops such as corn, wheat, soybeans, and apples. Large blocks of ice provided refrigeration in the freight cars, and they were replenished from an ice plant at one end of the rail yard.

You could mark time by the train whistles and factory horns that blew at precise intervals around the clock. These days, the trains no longer run through the center of town, but they do still pass along the edge of our property out in the country, and their sound is both nostalgic and comforting.

Skyline Grocery, a wholesale food company, was headquartered directly opposite the depot, with train tracks running right up to its loading docks. Today, that building is The Warehouse at 17th Street, which houses our catering kitchen, event space, mail-order operation, and offices. The old railroad tracks are preserved for posterity in the concrete foundation of a later addition to the building.

Factories right here in town made gloves, shoes, jackets, labels, and aluminum. A flour mill stood near the Illinois Central train station. Across the countryside, all around us, stretched orchards and farms. Coal mines dotted the landscape of every small Southern Illinois town back then. Mount Carbon and Replogle employed dozens of men from our town, and the pits left behind by strip mining became teen swimming holes.

People kept their money in Murphysboro and did business with one another, so there were plenty of jobs and a self-sustaining economy. Whether you were a factory worker or a carpenter, a banker or a grocer, you were able to comfortably raise a family and live a nice life.

═Mike═

A generation later, when I was growing up, the manufacturing was all but gone, with just the Lustour Corporation and Penn Aluminum factories remaining. The downtown was still lively and bustling, though, the epitome of 1970s and '80s small-town America, before the malls and big-box stores annihilated small local businesses. You could buy everything you needed right in town, and day-to-day shopping meant making your way to a number of different stores that lined three blocks: clothing stores, a shoe store, a jeweler, drugstores, the town bakery, and an assortment of other small shops.

We also had our own outposts of the old-school chain department/variety stores: Montgomery Ward, Ben Franklin, and Woolworth's—complete with soda fountain and swivel-y stools, where my middle-school friends, all long legs and pigtails, slurped many a fountain Coke and put a dent in our babysitting earnings buying fruity scented lip gloss, before hopping back on our bikes and heading out to spend the rest of our money on cute stationery at Jones' Card Shop—this was, of course, long before texting.

Of all my old haunts, the only ones that remain are the Farm Fresh Milk Store, where hours—and many pennies, nickels, and dimes—were spent in the candy section, and the Dairy Queen owned by Gary and Brenda Mills (yes, we're related).

More recently, the past few decades have been rough on Murphysboro, with a dramatically changing commerce and retail environment. Still, the town remains scrappy, spirited, and fiercely proud, and barbecue has played a big role in its recovery. The Murphysboro Barbecue Cook-Off that my daddy founded with his buddies Rob Williams and Pat Burke has attracted tourism and commerce to Murphysboro: Thousands of people are drawn to our town each September and all throughout the year.

Having had the good fortune to be products of two distinct periods in Murphysboro's history, we feel no less privileged to be part of its present and help write its next chapter. As 17th Street heads into its third decade, we look forward to continuing to feed barbecue pilgrims. Beyond that, we are in the process of rehabbing a classic 1940s building that in its previous lives housed a car dealership and an automotive parts store. It will become The Factory at 17th Street, where we will make and bottle our own sauces and dry rubs, as well as those of other barbecuers—thus completing a revolution of our region's commerce wheel. In the front will be a diner, where locals and visitors alike can enjoy breakfast, a cup of coffee, and small-town America as it lives on here in Murphysboro.

═Amy═

HIGH HOLY DAYS

FEED-A-CROWD DISHES FOR HOLIDAYS AND CELEBRATIONS

WHEN WE throw our own parties, here's how we do it. In this chapter, fun, festive, and familiar party food gets a good gussying-up.

For starters, straight-up classics are dressed up in party clothes: Grits and collards are layered into parfaits; fresh herbs and adobo blend with cream cheese to make a savory cheesecake; oysters go on the grill and gain a rockabilly flair; pork belly is smoked, glazed, and cubed into bites of pure hog heaven.

Moving on to the main event, nuanced seasonings, a kiss of smoke, and a fiery baptism bestow rock-star status upon all manner of prime feed-a-crowd cuts of meat. When it's time for backyard barbecue to go black-tie, these are your raise-the-roof recipes for revelry.

BELLY OF THE BEAST PORK BELLY BITES

MAKES ABOUT 60 PIECES

Lightly smoked, glazed, and cut into bite-size pieces, pork belly makes for a decadent appetizer. For the silkiest pork belly, source meat from a heritage breed such as Duroc or Cheshire, from a specialty purveyor like Compart Family Farms or Heritage Farms (see Resources, page 321). Conventional pork belly is also absolutely delicious. Either way, make sure to buy a skin-on piece so that the meat is protected as it cooks.

You can use different rubs, sauces, or a brine to vary the flavor profile of pork belly. One of our favorite variations is a pastrami-cured pork belly (see the variation on page 154), a tasty twist on the classic beef original. We've served pork belly meat at special events in tiny sliders, Vietnamese banh mi buns, tacos, and lettuce wraps.

If you can't find a small 4-pound cut of pork belly, simply cut a larger portion into 4-pound pieces and cook them all up together, using different rubs and sauces on each, if you like. You'll be happy to have extra.

4 pounds skin-on pork belly, in one piece

Cooking spray or vegetable oil

Pure Magic dry rub (page 29) or your choice

2 cups Apple City Barbecue Sauce (page 36) or your choice, warmed

5 to 10 pounds good-quality lump charcoal

1 small (8-inch) piece of apple wood or 2 store-bought chunks

String mop (see page 76)

Prep the belly: Spray the skin with cooking spray or rub with a paper towel dipped in vegetable oil—just enough to coat. Place skin side down and score the top of the entire belly into 1- to 1½-inch squares about three-quarters of the way through. Do not puncture the skin. Sprinkle the entire top and sides with dry rub. Set the meat on a baking sheet, skin side down, cover with plastic wrap, and refrigerate until you're ready to put it on the cooker.

Note: You can dust the meat with rub up to 1 hour prior to cooking, but if it sits much longer than that, the salt in the rub will begin to pull moisture from the meat.

Set up the cooker for indirect-heat smoking: Open the top and bottom vents. Pile 3 pounds of the charcoal in one half of the cooker, leaving the other half empty. Load a charcoal chimney one-quarter full of charcoal and light it. When

the coals in the chimney are glowing, dump them on top of the pile of charcoal in the cooker. Set the wood on top of the coals, replace the grate, and put the meat on the cooker, skin side down, over the side with no coals (the indirect cooking area). Close the lid.

Don't open the cooker for 1 hour, but keep a close eye on the temperature (see page 84 for how best to assess and monitor cooker temperature); when it reaches 230°, which might happen very quickly, close the vents about halfway so that less air comes in to feed the fire and the heat in the cooker rises slowly. Let the temperature climb to between 250° and 275° (see page 77 for how to determine your target temperature). **Maintain your target temperature for the duration of the cook.**

Throughout the entirety of the cook, be on the lookout for fluctuations in cooker temperature; whenever it dips more than 5° below target and opening the vents isn't sufficient to bring it back up, it's time to add a few hot coals. Reload and light the chimney as needed. If at any point the temperature climbs above your target by more than 5°, close the top and bottom vents further so that even less air comes in to feed the fire.

After an hour, open the lid and check the edge of the belly closest to the fire. If it looks like it's beginning to brown, rotate the meat, moving the side that is farthest away closest to the fire. Never flip the belly over; instead, continue rotating it so each of the four sides cooks evenly.

Use an instant-read thermometer to check the internal temperature of the meat: Insert the probe into the middle of the pork belly; you're looking for a slow and steady climb toward 205°.

Continue cooking the pork belly for 3 hours, checking the internal temperature of the meat every 30 minutes.

After 3 hours, check the meat for doneness: If the probe slides easily into the middle of the pork belly, the meat is nearly done. Continue to cook until the internal temperature reaches 204° or 205°. Use the string mop to glaze the belly with barbecue sauce, then sprinkle on a little more dry rub. Close the lid and cook for another few minutes, until the glaze sets. When the belly is done, you should be able to easily insert the tip of a knife into the meat and its internal temperature should be 205°.

Transfer the pork belly to a cutting board. Insert a very sharp knife between the skin and the meat, running it around the edges and through to the middle to separate the meat from the skin so that the meat rests on the skin but will easily lift away from it when served. Use the knife to follow the initial scores in the belly, cutting all the way through to, but not puncturing, the skin. Insert a toothpick into each square and serve as an appetizer.

Variation

PORK BELLY PASTRAMI

Make a half-batch of the brine preparation for Pastrami on the Pit (page 118), and brine the pork belly, per the method described, for 4 to 5 days. Coat the brined belly with a generous layer of Texas Forever Brisket Rub (page 30) or kosher salt and freshly ground black pepper, then cook according to the instructions above, omitting the glazing step. Cover the top of the pork belly pastrami with warm drained sauerkraut after cutting and prior to serving.

PRAISE THE LARD

SPINACH AND ARTICHOKE DIP

MAKES 12 TO 15 SERVINGS

Our version of the classic party dip—fancied up a bit with goat cheese, basil, and pine nuts, plus a dash of 17th Street Wing Sauce to keep it barbecue.

1 small garlic clove

¼ cup extra-virgin olive oil

¼ cup pine nuts

1 cup loosely packed fresh basil leaves

½ teaspoon kosher salt

¼ teaspoon freshly ground white pepper

8 ounces soft goat cheese, at room temperature

2½ cups freshly grated Parmesan cheese

1 large egg, lightly beaten

2 tablespoons 17th Street Wing Sauce (page 56)

One 14-ounce jar or can artichoke hearts, drained and chopped

One 10-ounce package frozen chopped spinach, thawed and drained

¼ cup panko bread crumbs, for topping

Crackers or tortilla chips, for serving

Preheat the oven to 350°, with a rack in the center.

Combine the garlic, olive oil, pine nuts, and basil in the bowl of a food processor and puree to a liquid. Scrape down the bowl, add the salt, pepper, and goat cheese, and pulse to blend. Scrape down the bowl once more, add 2 cups of the Parmesan cheese, and pulse just enough to mix. Transfer the mixture to a mixing bowl and fold in the egg, wing sauce, artichoke hearts, and spinach.

Scrape into a 1½-quart baking dish and top with bread crumbs and the remaining ½ cup Parmesan cheese. Bake for 25 to 30 minutes, until lightly browned and bubbling around the edges. Serve hot with the crackers or tortilla chips.

GRILLED STUFFED MUSHROOMS

MAKES ABOUT 15 APPETIZER SERVINGS

Mushrooms filled with our creamy spinach and artichoke dip and grilled until sizzling hot make for rich and creamy bites—perfect party food. They can also be cooked in the oven.

1 pound medium to large mushrooms

1½ cups Spinach and Artichoke Dip (page 155), mixed but not topped or baked (the remainder can be topped and baked as directed in the dip recipe, using a smaller baking dish)

Panko bread crumbs, for topping

Freshly grated Parmesan cheese, for topping

3 pounds good-quality lump charcoal, optional

Set up the cooker for direct cooking: Open the top and bottom vents. Pile 2 pounds of the charcoal in the bottom. Load a charcoal chimney one-quarter full of charcoal and light it. When the coals in the chimney are glowing, dump them on top of the pile of charcoal already in the cooker. Adjust the vents as necessary to establish a steady cooker temperature between 285° and 300°. (See pages 84 and 77 for how best to assess and monitor cooker temperature, and how to determine your target temperature.)

Line a baking sheet with paper towels or a kitchen towel. Remove and discard the mushroom stems. Wipe the mushrooms caps clean. Set the mushrooms on the prepared baking sheet and let them dry thoroughly.

Place a heaping teaspoon of the Spinach and Artichoke Dip in each mushroom cap and sprinkle with bread crumbs and Parmesan cheese.

Grill the mushrooms directly over the coals, with the lid closed, for about 15 minutes or until sizzling. Do not overcook or the mushrooms will shrivel. Alternatively, bake in a casserole dish or on a baking sheet in the oven at 350° for 25 to 30 minutes, until the tops are browned and sizzling. Arrange on a platter and serve hot.

SAVORY CHEESECAKE

MAKES ONE 8-INCH CAKE

While this impressive appetizer does present like a cheesecake—we love to display it on an elegant cake stand—it's consumed as a spread, lavished on assorted crackers and fresh fruit. One of our all-time favorite appetizers to feed a large cocktail party in high style, it can also be divided up into wedges and arrayed on separate serving trays. The recipe was first taught to us by our friend Tuffy Stone, an accomplished pitmaster, chef, and caterer. We switched up the cheeses and herbs to put our own spin on it, and once you've got the hang of the whole process, we encourage you to do the same.

2 teaspoons olive oil

¾ cup diced onions

1 teaspoon kosher salt

½ teaspoon freshly ground black pepper

Two 8-ounce packages cream cheese, at room temperature

6 ounces creamy goat cheese

1½ tablespoons pureed chipotle chiles in adobo sauce

3 ounces sun-dried tomatoes, finely chopped

2 tablespoons chopped fresh basil

6 large eggs

Crackers or fruit, for serving

Preheat the oven to 275°, with a rack in the center. Fill a 13-x-9-inch baking dish with water and place it on the lowest shelf in the oven. Lightly coat an 8-inch springform pan with cooking spray or brush with vegetable oil.

Coat a skillet with the olive oil and heat the pan over medium-high heat until the oil is shimmering. Add the onions, stir to coat, and season generously with salt and pepper. Reduce the heat to medium-low and spread the onions out evenly over the pan. Cook, stirring occasionally, for 10 to 15 minutes, until the onions are soft but not mushy and a rich brown color. Remove from the heat and set aside to cool.

Put the cream cheese in a large bowl and use an electric mixer on low speed just enough to break it up, then mix on medium-low speed just until soft.

Add the cooled onions, goat cheese, pureed chipotle, sun-dried tomatoes, and basil and mix on low speed until combined. Add the eggs one at a time, mixing gently until incorporated and using a flexible rubber spatula to scrape down the sides of the bowl, making sure all of the ingredients are well mixed. The mixture should be smooth.

(continued)

↓

Scrape the mixture into the prepared pan and set it on the center rack in the oven, above the pan of water. Bake for 1 hour, or until the cheesecake is set and a tester inserted into the middle comes out clean. Cool to room temperature, then cover and transfer to the refrigerator to chill overnight.

To serve, run a thin knife around the edge of the cake, then remove the pan's ring. Set the whole cake on a large serving platter or cake stand, or slice the cake into wedges and place on serving dishes. Serve with crackers and fruit.

STRAWBERRY AND GOAT CHEESE SALAD

MAKES 6 SERVINGS

Homemade dressing elevates any salad, and it's what makes this simple, fresh side so delicious. A little sweet, a little tangy, it's a surprising blend of just three ingredients, and it's the perfect complement to the strawberries, pecans, and goat cheese. We serve this salad at all sorts of catered affairs and special events. It's one of the most requested recipes by guests and other restaurateurs who attend our classes. We've held onto the secret until now.

DRESSING

1 cup mayonnaise (we use Hellmann's)

½ cup packed light brown sugar

3 tablespoons apple cider vinegar

8 cups field greens, washed and dried

1 pint strawberries, washed, hulled, and sliced

½ cup creamy goat cheese (one 4-ounce package)

½ cup toasted pecans

For the dressing: Combine the mayonnaise, sugar, and vinegar in a blender and blend until smooth. Add a small bit of water to thin as desired. Decant into a squeeze bottle.

Add the greens and strawberries to a large bowl. Using a fork, break up the goat cheese and sprinkle over the greens. Just before serving, drizzle the salad with the dressing, then sprinkle with the pecans. Serve family-style on a big platter or individual portions on chilled plates.

GRITS AND COLLARD PARFAITS

MAKES 12 PARFAITS

Mason jar parfaits made from layers of creamy stone-ground grits, slow-cooked from scratch, and cane sugar–spiked collard greens make a portable party food. The potlikker from the collards drips down into the grits and combines with their nutty texture to take these simple parfaits to the next level. We buy local varieties of grits whenever we travel in the Carolinas; they each have a different texture and tooth. See the Resources section (page 321) for our favorites. One of our secrets to great grits is substituting homemade turkey or chicken stock for half of the water for depth and richness. If your stock is very salty, adjust the amount of salt in this recipe.

Note: Proper seasoning is essential for tasty grits, but once cooked the grits won't absorb salt, so make sure to salt the water or add the salt and grits together at the outset.

1 cup stone-ground grits	1 teaspoon kosher salt	12 pieces Legendary Baby Back Ribs (page 88) or Lacquered Bacon (page 50), for garnish (optional)
2 cups homemade turkey or chicken stock, plus more as needed	½ teaspoon freshly ground black pepper	
4 tablespoons (½ stick) unsalted butter	3 cups Brisket-Seasoned Collards (page 220), lightly drained, steaming hot	12 half-pint mason jars

Pour the grits into a large bowl, cover with 2 cups water, and stir. Allow to settle for 5 minutes, then skim off any floating hulls and chaff with a small fine-mesh sieve. Drain.

Bring the stock, 2 tablespoons of the butter, and the salt to a boil in a 4-quart heavy-bottom saucepan. Gradually add the grits, stirring constantly with a wooden spoon. Reduce the heat and cook at a low simmer, partially covered, stirring frequently and adding stock as needed to prevent sticking, until the liquid is absorbed and the grits are creamy and tender, 30 to 40 minutes. Stir in the remaining 2 tablespoons butter and the pepper.

Layer ¼ cup of the grits in each mason jar. Top with ¼ cup of the collards. Garnish with a rib bone or a piece of Lacquered Bacon, if desired.

OYSTERS ON THE GRILL

MAKES 36

This recipe will be delicious with any kind of oysters, so long as they are very fresh. My favorites come from Island Creek Oysters, located just 30 minutes from my Boston outpost (see Resources, page 321). We created a rockabilly take on grilled oysters Rockefeller, using both our collards and spinach-artichoke dip. They're splashed with mignonette made with Hog Wash and dotted with hot sauce. —Amy

¼ cup minced red onion

1 cup Hog Wash Vinegar Splash (page 40)

3 dozen oysters, shucked and set back in bottom shells (flat top shells discarded)

½ cup Brisket-Seasoned Collards (page 220)

6 slices crispy cooked bacon, minced

½ cup Spinach and Artichoke Dip (page 155), mixed but not topped or baked

Freshly grated Parmesan cheese, for topping

Hot sauce (your choice), for serving

Lemon wedges, for serving

Rock salt, for cooking and serving

3 pounds good-quality charcoal

For the mignonette, add the onion to the Hog Wash in a serving bowl. Cover and set aside until you're ready to serve. Line a serving platter with rock salt.

Prep the oysters: Line 2 rimmed baking sheets with a layer of rock salt. Shuck the oysters. Loosen each oyster, setting it back in the bottom shell and carefully preserving the liquor, and nestle in the rock salt. Discard the top shell.

Set up the cooker for direct cooking: Open the top and bottom vents. Pile 2 pounds of the charcoal in the bottom. Load a charcoal chimney one-quarter full of charcoal and light it. When the coals in the chimney are glowing, dump them on top of the pile of charcoal already in the cooker. Adjust the vents as necessary to establish a steady temperature between 285° and 300°.

In 18 of the oysters, carefully dollop a spoonful of collards and top with a pinch of crispy bacon. In the remaining 18 oysters, dab in a spoonful of spinach-artichoke dip and top with a bit of Parmesan cheese.

Set the oysters, in their half shells, directly on the grill, over the coals. Close the lid and cook for 5 to 8 minutes, or until sizzling.

Taking care not to slosh out the liquor, use tongs to transfer the shells to the prepared platter. Serve immediately with the mignonette, hot sauce, and lemon wedges.

MAJESTIC PRIME RIB

MAKES 18 TO 20 SERVINGS, MORE IF SLICED THIN

Slowly pit-cooked for a beautifully smoky, decadently rich interior clad in a savory crusty char, this impressive roast is the star of any meal. Prime and choice grades are both delicious, but prime will be markedly more marbled—truly a cut above. Serve the roast with classic horseradish cream or bright, fresh, garlicky chimichurri sauce.

Note: After you take the roast off the cooker, the internal temperature will rise while the meat rests—and the higher the cooking temperature has been, the longer the meat will continue to cook in its resting state. So you can be confident that the end pieces will be more done for folks who prefer their prime rib that way, while slices from the middle will have a perfectly rare center.

One 13- to 14-pound boneless prime rib roast (prime or choice)	Horseradish Cream (recipe follows) or Chimichurri Sauce (page 173), for serving	8 to 10 pounds good-quality lump charcoal
Texas Forever Brisket Rub (page 30)		2 small (8-inch) pieces of apple wood or post oak or 4 store-bought chunks

Prep the meat: Remove the outer membrane from the top of the roast and the excess fat from the roll of the roast.

At least 20 minutes before cooking, sprinkle the entire piece of meat generously all over with dry rub. Set the roast on a baking sheet, loosely cover with plastic wrap, and refrigerate until you're ready to put it on the cooker.

Note: You can dust the meat with rub up to 1 hour prior to cooking, but if it sits much longer than that, the salt in the rub will begin to pull moisture from the meat.

Set up the cooker for indirect-heat smoking: Open the top and bottom vents. Pile 3 pounds of the charcoal in one half of the cooker, leaving the other half empty. Load a charcoal chimney one-quarter full of charcoal and light it. When the coals in the chimney are glowing, dump them on top of the pile of charcoal in the cooker. Set half the wood on top of the coals, replace the grate, and put the meat on the cooker, bottom (flatter) side down, over the side with no coals (the indirect cooking area). Close the lid.

Don't open the cooker for 1 hour, but keep a close eye on the temperature (see page 84 for how best to assess and monitor cooker temperature); when it reaches 275°, which might happen very quickly, close the vents about halfway so that

less air comes in to feed the fire and the heat in the cooker rises slowly. Let the temperature climb to between 285° and 300° (see page 77 for how to determine your target temperature). **Maintain your target temperature for the duration of the cook.**

Throughout the entirety of the cook, be on the lookout for fluctuations in cooker temperature; whenever it dips more than 5° below target and opening the vents isn't sufficient to bring it back up, it's time to add a few hot coals. Reload and light the chimney as needed. If at any point the temperature climbs above your target by more than 5°, close the top and bottom vents further so that even less air comes in to feed the fire.

After an hour, open the lid and check the edge of the meat closest to the fire. If it looks like it's beginning to brown, rotate the meat, moving the side that is farthest away closest to the fire. Never flip the roast over; instead continue rotating it so each of the four sides cooks evenly. Use an instant-read thermometer to check the temperature of the meat: Insert the probe into the middle of the roast; you're looking for a slow and steady climb toward 110°.

After the first round of wood burns, add the rest.

After the meat has been on the cooker for 3½ to 4 hours, check for doneness: If the probe slides in easily, the meat is nearly done. For rare, take the meat off the cooker when the internal temperature reaches between 110° and 115°; for medium-rare, 118° to 120°. Set it on a cutting board to rest, uncovered, for 20 to 30 minutes before carving.

Carve into 1-inch-thick slices (thinner for sandwiches) and serve with Horseradish Cream and/or Chimichurri Sauce alongside.

Horseradish Cream

MAKES ABOUT 1½ CUPS

Cold and creamy, with a zippy edge of horseradish, this is the classic condiment for prime rib and other rich cuts of beef. Buy a fresh jar of horseradish or use one that's less than 4 weeks old, as even preserved horseradish begins to lose its zing after a month or so.

1 cup sour cream

6 tablespoons drained prepared horseradish

2 tablespoons chopped fresh chives

2 tablespoons mayonnaise (we use Hellmann's)

2 teaspoons Dijon mustard

½ teaspoon kosher salt

½ teaspoon freshly ground black pepper

Whisk together all the ingredients in a small bowl until thoroughly combined. Chill for 2 hours prior to use. The sauce keeps, covered and refrigerated, for 1 week.

COFFEE-CRUSTED BEEF TENDERLOIN

MAKES ABOUT 8 SERVINGS; MORE IF SLICED THINNER

A whisper of smoke and charcoal flavor takes classic, buttery beef tenderloin to a new level. This is the perfect celebratory, feed-a-crowd food. Tenderloin also happens to be one of the easier cuts to master, so it's an excellent choice if you're still honing your smoking skills but want to throw a party. You can serve the tenderloin sliced, as an entrée, or cut very thin to make little sandwiches. Either way, accompany with a variety of barbecue sauces, chimichurri, horseradish cream, or mustard.

Note: There is hardly any fat in this cut of meat, so it's best cooked to rare; after you take the tenderloin off the cooker, the internal temperature will rise while the meat rests—and the higher the cooking temperature has been, the longer it will continue to cook in its resting state. So you can be confident that the end pieces will be more done for folks who prefer their meat that way, while slices from the middle will have a perfectly rare center.

One 5- to 6-pound beef tenderloin

½ cup Java Jolt dry rub (page 31)

Chimichurri Sauce (recipe follows), Horseradish Cream (page 169), or your choice of barbecue sauce or mustard, for serving

8 to 10 pounds good-quality lump charcoal

2 small (8-inch) pieces of apple wood or 4 store-bought chunks

Prep the meat: Remove the outer membrane (silverskin) from the tenderloin. At least 30 minutes before cooking, sprinkle generously all over with dry rub. Set the tenderloin on a baking sheet, loosely cover it with plastic wrap, and refrigerate until you're ready to put it on the cooker.

Note: You can dust the tenderloin with rub up to 1 hour prior to cooking, but if it sits much longer than that, the salt in the rub will begin to pull moisture from the meat.

Set up the cooker for indirect-heat smoking: Open the top and bottom vents. Pile 3 pounds of the charcoal in one half of the cooker, leaving the other half empty. Load a charcoal chimney one-quarter full of charcoal and light it. When the coals in the chimney are glowing, dump them on top of the pile of charcoal already

in the cooker. Set half the wood on top of the coals, replace the grate, and put the tenderloin over the side with no coals (the indirect cooking area). Close the lid.

Don't open the cooker for 1 hour, but keep a close eye on the temperature (see page 84 for how best to assess and monitor cooker temperature); when it reaches 200°, which might happen very quickly, close the vents about halfway so that less air comes in to feed the fire and the heat in the cooker rises slowly. Let the temperature climb to between 225° and 250° (see page 77 for how to determine your target temperature). **Maintain your target temperature for the duration of the cook.**

Throughout the entirety of the cook, be on the lookout for fluctuations in cooker temperature; whenever it dips more than 5° below target and opening the vents isn't sufficient to bring it back up, it's time to add a few hot coals. Reload and light the chimney as needed. If at any point the temperature climbs above your target by more than 5°, close the top and bottom vents further so that even less air comes in to feed the fire.

After an hour, open the lid and check the edge of the meat that is closest to the fire. If it looks like it's beginning to brown, rotate the meat, moving the side that is farthest away closest to the fire. Never flip the tenderloin over; instead continue rotating it to brown evenly all over.

After the meat has been on the cooker for 1½ to 2 hours, use an instant-read thermometer to check the internal temperature of the meat: Insert the probe into the middle of the tenderloin; you're looking for a slow and steady climb toward 130°. After the first round of wood burns, add the rest.

At the 3- to 3½-hour mark, check for doneness: If the thermometer probe slides in easily, the meat is nearly done. For rare, take the meat off the cooker when the internal temperature reads 130°. Set it on a cutting board to rest, uncovered, for 10 to 20 minutes before carving. Slice ¼ inch thick, thinner for sandwiches.

Serve with Chimichurri Sauce, Horseradish Cream, barbecue sauce, or mustard.

Chimichurri Sauce

MAKES ABOUT 1 CUP

This sauce is vivid in both color and flavor, zippy with garlic and parsley.

1 cup packed fresh flat-leaf parsley leaves

8 garlic cloves, minced

¾ cup extra virgin olive oil

½ cup red wine vinegar

2 tablespoons fresh lemon juice

1 tablespoon diced red onion

1 teaspoon minced fresh oregano

1 teaspoon coarsely ground black pepper

½ teaspoon kosher salt

Combine all the ingredients in a food processor or blender and puree to a pourable consistency. Transfer to a bowl. Cover and let stand up to 1 hour at room temperature. The sauce can be made up to 2 hours ahead, but is best used the same day. Serve at room temperature.

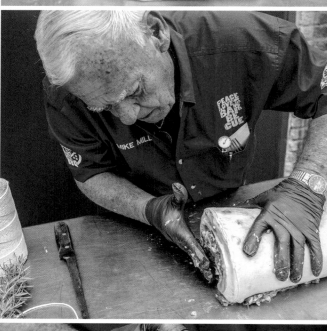

PORK BELLY PORCHETTA

MAKES 10 TO 12 SERVINGS

A traditional porchetta requires a deboned suckling pig, which can be a daunting and labor-intensive task. Replicating the recipe with a pork belly is much easier and equally delicious. The result is a real showstopper: a gleaming, glossy roll of pork, fragrant with herbs, with layers of sausage, melting fat, and belly meat visible on each end. Crispy bits of skin, moist pork, and well-seasoned sausage in each and every bite make for some mighty tasty eating.

Note: Make the brine a day in advance so it has time to thoroughly steep and chill. After that, the meat needs to soak in the brine, undisturbed, for 5 to 7 days. You'll need a 5-gallon brining bucket or a food-grade plastic storage container large enough to accommodate both the meat and enough brine to cover it by an inch or so. You may need to take a shelf out of your refrigerator to make room. Duration is also crucial; if the meat isn't brined long enough, it won't take on the full flavor. Note that the process takes seven-plus days: one day for the brine to chill, at least five days for the meat to soak, and a day for the cook.

BRINE

1 pound sugar

1 pound salt

One 10- to 12-pound skin-on pork belly, in one piece

HERB SEASONING

½ cup extra virgin olive oil

1 bunch fresh flat-leaf parsley (1½ cups loosely packed leaves)

6 fresh sage leaves

1 tablespoon fresh rosemary leaves

3 garlic cloves, peeled

3 tablespoons ground fennel seeds

Grated zest of 1 lemon

1 tablespoon Dijon mustard

Kosher salt and coarsely ground black pepper

2 pounds bulk fresh pork sausage or sweet Italian sausage

Sprigs of rosemary or another herb

Large stainless-steel stockpot

5-gallon brining bucket or food-grade plastic container large enough to fit meat submerged in brine (see page 75)

A plate and a weight to help hold the meat down in case it floats to the top (it must be submerged; a brick or large rock works well)

10 to 15 pounds good-quality lump charcoal (we use Royal Oak)

4 small (8-inch) pieces of apple wood or 8 store-bought chunks

Make room in your refrigerator to fit the large container in which you'll be brining the pork belly.

(continued)

↓

For the brine: Mix the salt and sugar in a large stockpot. Add ½ gallon hot water and stir to dissolve. Add 2 gallons cold water and stir to combine. Place the brine in the refrigerator until well chilled.

Pierce the meat side of the belly all over with a two-pronged meat fork, being careful not to pierce the skin. Put the pork belly in the plastic container and pour the brine over the top, covering by at least 1 inch. Set a plate and a weight on top of the meat to keep it submerged. Cover the container with a lid or plastic wrap, then transfer to the refrigerator and let sit undisturbed for 5 to 7 days.

For the herb seasoning: Pulse all the ingredients in a food processor to a coarse puree. Scrape the mixture into a bowl and set aside.

Take the pork belly out of the brine and pat it dry. Lay it out skin side down, generously season it with salt and pepper, then spread onto the entire belly the herb mixture followed by the sausage. Tightly roll the pork belly into a cylinder,

continually pushing in the sausage that squeezes out from the ends. Lay the herb sprigs along the top and tie the roll with butcher's twine about every 1½ inches.

Set up the cooker for indirect-heat smoking: Open the top and bottom vents. Pile 3 pounds of the charcoal in one half of the cooker, leaving the other half empty. Load a charcoal chimney one-quarter full of charcoal and light it. When the coals in the chimney are glowing, dump them on top of the pile of charcoal in the cooker. Set half the wood on top of the coals, replace the grate, and put the porchetta over the side with no coals (the indirect cooking area). Close the lid.

Keep a close eye on the temperature (see page 84 for how best to assess and monitor cooker temperature); when it reaches 225°, which might happen very quickly, close the vents about halfway so that less air comes in to feed the fire and the heat in the cooker rises slowly. Let the temperature climb to between 250° and 275° (see page 77 for how to determine your target temperature). **Maintain your target temperature for the duration of the cook.**

Throughout the entirety of the cook, be on the lookout for fluctuations in cooker temperature; whenever it dips more than 5° below target and opening the vents isn't sufficient to bring it back up, it's time to add a few hot coals. Reload and light the chimney as needed. If at any point the temperature climbs above your target by more than 5°, close the top and bottom vents further so that even less air comes in to feed the fire.

After the porchetta has been on the cooker for 1½ to 2 hours, periodically check the edges of the meat closest to the fire. Rotate the meat as needed to brown evenly, but never flip it over. Use an instant-read thermometer to check the internal temperature of the meat: Insert the probe into the middle of the porchetta; you're looking for a slow and steady climb toward 155° in the center. As the wood burns throughout the cook, add the pieces from the chimney until the meat reaches between 135° and 140°.

After the 4-hour mark, begin checking for doneness: When the center of the porchetta is between 150° and 155°, remove it from the cooker. Set it on a cutting board to rest, uncovered, for 10 to 20 minutes before removing the strings and carving into ½-inch-thick slices.

APRICOT-GLAZED PIT-SMOKED PORK LOIN

MAKES 10 TO 12 SERVINGS; MORE IF SLICED THINNER

Lean pork cuts, such as a loin, are where heritage breeds like Duroc, Cheshire, Berkshire, and Red Wattle will truly be superior, bringing a marked difference in flavor and moisture content. An apricot glaze adds just a little sweetness; the delicate, smoke-kissed pork is really the star of the show. Just as with pork chops, we cook this to a perfect pink. An internal temperature between 150° and 155° is ideal.

One 8- to 10-pound pork loin (preferably Duroc or other well-marbled heritage breed)

Mustard Slather (page 31)

Texas Forever Brisket Rub (page 30), or your choice

Apricot Glaze (page 41), warm

8 to 10 pounds good-quality lump charcoal

2 small (8-inch) pieces of apple wood or 4 store-bought chunks

String mop (see page 76)

Prep the meat: Remove the outer membrane (silverskin) from the loin and trim the fat cap to about ¼ inch. Up to 4 hours before cooking, coat the entire piece of meat with a thin layer of Mustard Slather and sprinkle generously all over with dry rub. Set it on a baking sheet, loosely cover it with plastic wrap, and refrigerate until you're ready to put it on the cooker.

Note: You can dust the loin with rub up to 4 hours prior to cooking, but if it sits much longer than that, the salt in the rub will begin to pull moisture from the meat.

Set up the cooker for indirect-heat smoking: Open the top and bottom vents. Pile 3 pounds of the charcoal in one half of the cooker, leaving the other half empty. Load a charcoal chimney one-quarter full of charcoal and light it. When the coals in the chimney are glowing, dump them on top of the pile of charcoal already in the cooker. Set half the wood on top of the coals, replace the grate, and put the loin over the side with no coals (the indirect cooking area). Close the lid.

Don't open the lid for 1 hour, but keep a close eye on the temperature (see page 84 for how best to assess and monitor cooker temperature); when it reaches 200°, which might happen very quickly, close the vents about halfway so that less air comes in to feed the fire and the heat in the cooker rises slowly. Let the temperature climb to between 225° and 250° (see page 77 for how to determine

your target temperature). **Maintain your target temperature for the duration of the cook.**

Throughout the entirety of the cook, be on the lookout for fluctuations in cooker temperature; whenever it dips more than 5° below target and opening the vents isn't sufficient to bring it back up, it's time to add a few hot coals. Reload and light the chimney as needed. If at any point the temperature climbs above your target by more than 5°, close the top and bottom vents further so that even less air comes in to feed the fire.

After the meat has been on the cooker for 1 hour, open the lid and check the edge of the meat that is closest to the fire. If it looks like it's beginning to brown, rotate the meat, moving the side that is farthest away closest to the fire. Never flip the loin over; instead continue rotating it to brown evenly all over. Use an instant-read thermometer to check the internal temperature of the meat: Insert the probe into the middle of the loin; you're looking for a slow and steady climb toward 150°. As the wood burns throughout the cook, continue to add the other pieces until the meat reaches between 135° and 140°.

After 1½ to 2 more hours, check for doneness: If the probe slides easily into the middle of the pork loin, the meat is nearly done. When the internal temperature reads between 150° and 155°, use a string mop to give it a thin coat of Apricot Glaze, then close the lid for just a minute to let it dry a bit. Mop with a second thin coat and take the meat off the cooker. Set the loin on a cutting board, uncovered, to rest for 10 minutes before carving. Slice ¼ inch thick, thinner if desired.

CHERRY SODA–GLAZED HAM

MAKES ABOUT 20 SERVINGS

Scout out local or regional soda, and farmstand cherry preserves in your area to make a glaze that adds a unique touch to a party-size ham, a fantastic centerpiece for any holiday or party table. Ham is an easy cut to cook outdoors and the perfect meat to have on hand when you need to feed a crowd. Many hams purchased at the market are already cured; you can also purchase an uncured or "green" ham, which will take a few more hours to cook.

One 14- to 16-pound boneless ham

Cheerwine Glaze (page 41), warm

8 to 10 pounds good-quality lump charcoal

2 small (8-inch) pieces of apple wood or 4 store-bought chunks

String mop (see page 76)

Score the surface of the ham with shallow diamond-shaped or square cuts.

Set up the cooker for indirect-heat smoking: Open the top and bottom vents. Pile 3 pounds of the charcoal in one half of the cooker, leaving the other half empty. Load a charcoal chimney one quarter full of charcoal and light it. When the coals in the chimney are glowing, dump them on top of the pile of charcoal already in the cooker. Set half the wood on top of the coals, replace the grate, and put the ham over the side with no coals (the indirect cooking area). Close the lid.

Don't open the lid for 1 hour, but keep a close eye on the temperature (see page 84 for how best to assess and monitor cooker temperature); when it reaches 220°, which might happen very quickly, close the vents about halfway so that less air comes in to feed the fire and the heat in the cooker rises slowly. Let the temperature climb to between 225° and 250° (see page 77 for how to determine your target temperature). **Maintain your target temperature for the duration of the cook.**

Throughout the entirety of the cook, be on the lookout for fluctuations in cooker temperature. If the temperature in the cooker dips more than 5° below your target and opening the vents isn't sufficient to bring it back up, you will need to add a few hot coals. Reload and light the chimney as needed. If at any point the temperature climbs above your target by more than 5°, close the top and bottom vents further so that even less air comes in to feed the fire.

(continued)
↓

After the meat has been on the cooker for 1 hour, open the lid and check the edge of the meat that is closest to the fire. If it looks like it's beginning to brown, rotate the meat, moving the side that is farthest away closest to the fire. Never flip the ham over; instead continue rotating it to brown evenly all over. Use an instant-read thermometer to check the temperature of the meat: Insert the probe into the middle of the ham; you're looking for a slow and steady climb toward 145°. As the wood burns throughout the cook, continue to add the other pieces until the meat reaches between 135° and 140°.

After 2 to 2½ more hours, check the meat for temperature. When the internal temperature reads between 143° and 145°, use a string mop to give it a thin coat of Cheerwine Glaze, then close the lid for just a minute to let it dry a bit. Mop with a second thin coat and remove from the cooker. Set the ham on a cutting board to rest, uncovered, for 20 to 30 minutes prior to carving. Slice ¼ inch thick.

HELPING HANDS

Looking back, I don't know what would have become of us had it not been for the neighbors, family friends, and people from church who stepped up and stepped in and helped take care of my sisters and me when my daddy, Leon, died in 1949 at the age of forty-two. I was only seven, and Mama Faye was left with three children still at home: me, my twelve-year-old sister Jeanette, and my baby sister Mary Pat, who was just six months old.

Of course my brothers Landess and Bob, twelve and thirteen years older than me, played a large role in raising me. Bob taught me to hunt and fish when he was home from college on weekends, and when he moved back to Murphysboro, Mama Faye would call him to come over and give me a spanking when necessary. I spent a lot of time on the weekends with Landess, tagging along as he built his own wholesale business and learning a lot about wheeling and dealing.

However, Bob and Landess were married and had households of their own to tend to, so there was only so much they could do. Other folks, though, played a crucial role. It seemed like somebody was always including me in an activity or taking me along on a family outing.

One of the families that glow in my memory is the Grammers, who had me stay with them for the first few weeks right after Daddy died and who continued to welcome me into their home well into my teen years. We knew them from church, and their son,

Jim, was my age and a good friend. He and I were in Cub Scouts together, and Mr. Grammer was our pack leader. He worked as a salesman for a plumbing company in town. He was a handy guy who did a lot of woodworking in his spare time, so Jim and I were always helping him make something. He also cooked outside a lot and that made me feel good because that's what I was used to at home. He didn't barbecue low and slow like my daddy, but he grilled meat and that tasted good to me. Mrs. Grammer did a lot of baking, which I certainly appreciated.

When I was thirteen, I got a job delivering newspapers. The lady in charge of assigning routes knew me from church, and she gave me a prime downtown circuit, covering all of the businesses on Walnut Street. I had to walk—I couldn't ride a bike and toss papers onto porches like most of the other kids. I had to go into each store and hand the newspaper right to the shop owner. I had that same route for three years, and got to know all of my customers pretty well. At the time, I thought the biggest advantage was that most of those business-owning folks paid six months or a year at a time and, come Christmas, they all gave me nice gifts. But when I moved back to Murphysboro in my early twenties, many of those people were still in business, and being known as their longtime paperboy helped paved the way to my establishing myself as a fellow businessman.

═Mike═

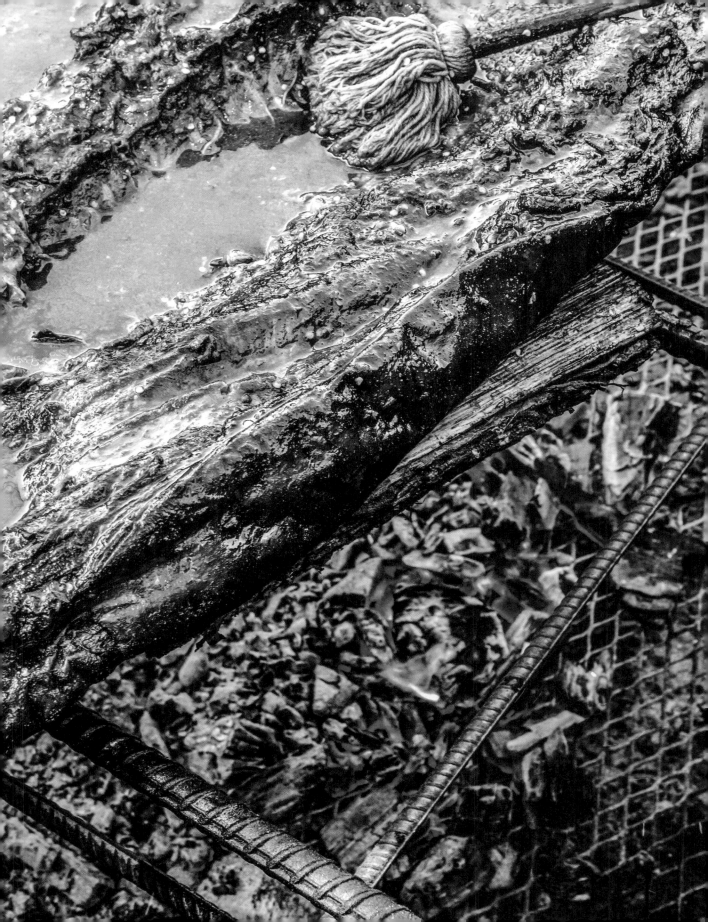

PRAISE THE LARD

DIY WHOLE HOG EXTRAVAGANZA

CAN THERE be any occasion more celebratory than a pig pickin'? Be it a backyard picnic or a blowout wedding bash, whole hog makes it an extravaganza, with an amazing centerpiece that provides unparalleled festivity, fellowship, and feast.

This time-honored barbecue ritual is so important to us that we not only serve up a whole hog at our restaurants on a weekly basis, we cart the cooked hog—in all her burnished glory—into the dining room and pull off the meat to order.

Time stands still during the 20 to 24 hours it takes to prep and cook a hog, and the conversations and libations you share around the burn barrel, late into the night, are seared into your memory forever. There's something eminently sacred about the entire process of this most primitive meat-meets-fire rite.

On the following pages, we walk you through every step of cooking a whole hog, including the preliminaries of ordering a "pretty pig" and the advantages of seeking out a heritage breed. We get you up close and personal with the mechanics of prepping and positioning the massive beast—squatted versus splayed—and getting her into the cooker. And we take you through the cardinal rules of fire management, sharing pitmaster secrets for setting up the presentation area and the finer points of chopping and mixing meat from various parts of the hog to make the most delectable sandwiches.

Go forth, armed and ready with the knowledge, tools, and confidence to take on the whole hog challenge. And may the barbecue gods be with you.

Go Whole Hog, Baby *193*

Whole Hog: Microcosm of Regional American Barbecue

Whole hogs are cooked daily or weekly in parts of North and South Carolina, western Tennessee, and Southern Illinois. The wood, spice, salt, and style of cooking are distinct in each area. In western Tennessee, whole hogs are cooked on their backs, using hickory wood and dry rub, and served with a red barbecue sauce. In North Carolina, hogs are simply seasoned with iodized salt, cooked over red or white oak, on the belly and back (to blister the skin), and chopped with a liberal dousing of vinegar. South Carolina is much the same as North Carolina, replacing vinegar with a spicy red sauce. In Southern Illinois, the hogs are cooked with a combination of apple or wild cherry and pecan woods, on their backs or in a squatted position, with dry rub, vinegar sauce, and a red barbecue sauce.

HERITAGE HOGS

Commodity hogs are on the menu each week at 17th Street. For contests and special events, we prefer heritage hogs, which cost more than twice as much per pound. Raised under humane conditions on family farms, heritage hogs are prized for their high fat content and rich flavor. Berkshire, Chester White, Duroc, Mangalitsa, and Red Wattle are a few of the delicious breeds available from family farms and specialty producers across the country (see Resources, page 321).

Ordering a Hog

Specify a "dressed" hog when you order. This means the pig will have the hair and bristles removed from the skin, the belly slit open and cleared of all the internal organs, and the eyelids cut off. If you want the head on the hog for presentation purposes, be sure to request that; otherwise you may find yourself with a headless hog. A dressed hog weighs about 70 percent of its live weight, so ordering it dressed is a better deal. If you remove the organs yourself, you're paying 30 percent more for the hog.

For the restaurant, we always order a 150-pound hog, which will weigh between 150 and 170 pounds; the delivered weight is never precise. The larger the hog, the longer it will take to cook—and the more help you will need to heave it onto the cooker and then back off once it's cooked. (Hogs are heavy, dead weight.) For cooking at home, a 100- to 130-pound hog is a good size. A 100-pound hog will yield about 40 pounds of pork, enough to make around 120 to 130 sandwiches.

If you are going to cook the pig in a squatted position, request a short-coupled hog, referring to the length from the nose to the tail. A short-coupled hog will fit better inside an Ole Hickory Double-Wide CTO and other insulated cookers. If the hog is too long, simply saw off the legs and/or head with a meat saw. Cook those alongside the hog for serving, use as seasoning meat, or discard.

TWO WAYS TO COOK A HOG

There are two ways to cook a hog: splayed on its back (photo, page 196) or squatted in a military-crawl position (photo, page 199).

In our restaurant, we usually squat the hog. We do this for a few different reasons. Aesthetically, it's a prettier presentation. One side is garnished and pristine for the public to see, and we pull the meat off the other side by cutting out a section of the skin and reaching inside. This allows the hog to stay fresh and hot for

several hours while we're serving it. A hog that's cooked on its back can be pulled in front of guests as well, but the meat will not stay warm quite as long. Whichever way you cook and serve it, a crowd always gathers when you're pickin' a pig.

A splayed hog starts out belly down, to absorb smoke into the meat, and is flipped over during the cook. A squatted hog remains in the same position throughout.

Our Favorite Pits for Cooking Whole Hog

For cooking whole hog, we recommend any of the following models (for ordering information, see Resources, page 321). You can cook a hog squatted or splayed in any of these pits.

Old-fashioned brick pit You can build one of these yourself using concrete blocks (there are instructions all over the internet).

Ole Hickory CTO-DW This is a lifetime piece of equipment and you can cook whole hogs as well as other barbecue on this cooker. It's well insulated and holds a consistent temperature for 2 to 4 hours at a time, thus requiring less monitoring and less charcoal and wood. A fan gently moves the smoke and air around the cooking chamber and it holds moisture, requiring no water pan. We use these in our restaurants and we also cook our prize-winning Memphis in May whole hogs on this pit. This pit is fired with charcoal with sticks of wood placed on top to smolder. From $9,500.

BQ Grills Charcoal Wood-Fired Pig Cooker Designed by Sam Jones of Skylight Inn and Sam Jones BBQ in North Carolina, using the same principles as the brick pits they use at their restaurants. This pit is fed with live coals from a burn barrel. $2,500 to $4,400.

Backwoods Smoker The Whole Hog Many champion competition cookers use this well-insulated smoker with a carousel rack for turning and displaying the hog. This pit is fired with charcoal, with sticks of wood placed on top to smolder. From $9,930.

Peg Leg Porker Whole Hog Cooker An indirect, forced-convection, triple-walled vertical smoker designed and built to order by Carey Bringle. He won third place whole hog at Memphis in May on this pit's inaugural competition cook. The larger model will hold two hogs at a time. This pit is fired with charcoal, with sticks of wood placed on top to smolder. $5,000 to $12,000.

Staging a Whole Hog

For presenting and serving whole hog, we have found that a good base is a six-foot collapsible table equipped with leg extenders to bring the height up to a more comfortable level (see page 76). Hog pickin' is messy, so cover the table with a disposable plastic tablecloth. And the hog will be heavy; you won't want to move the hog or the table once you get started, so plan accordingly.

TIME AND TEMPERATURE

While doneness will always be measured by temperature, not time, here are some basic guidelines, based on weight and cooking at a steady temperature between 250° and 275°.

Dressed Weight	Cooking Time
100 pounds	12 to 14 hours
125 pounds	14 to 16 hours
150 pounds	18 to 20 hours
175 pounds	20 to 22 hours
200 pounds	22 to 24 hours

GO WHOLE HOG, BABY

From a financial perspective, there's not a lot to like about cooking whole hogs. In the restaurant business, you don't really get enough meat and money to justify the work that you put into it.

We do it anyway. There are a lot of people out there who have no idea where their food actually comes from. We get a huge kick out of seeing children and adults watch the pig being wheeled into the dining room. They come over to examine it and ask questions and have their picture taken with it. We look at it as an educational opportunity, an important part of barbecue culture that needs to live on. We want those families to share in the experience each week and continue the tradition by bringing their children and grandchildren to 17th Street to see the hog.

Various aspects of the cooking method depend upon how you position your hog—splayed versus squatted—so the following instructions are tailored accordingly. Cooking a whole hog is a group project—you'll want to tag team with a buddy or two.

One 100-pound dressed hog

Mustard Slather (page 31)

Dry rub (your choice)

Hog Wash Vinegar Splash (page 40)

Lettuce, kale, other vegetables, and/or fruit, for presentation (optional)

Apple or other decoration of your choice, for presentation

Barbecue sauce (your choice), for serving

White bread or potato rolls, for sandwiches (optional)

Meat saw (don't use a Sawzall; it creates tiny bone shards that can end up in the meat)

Hatchet

Rubber mallet

Small piece of wood for the pig's mouth

Rolled up 13-x-10-x-5-inch piece of chicken wire or thin steel diamond mesh if cooking the hog in a squatted position

Small bucket of salt water and a rag, for washing a squatted hog

Burn barrel (see page 75)

½ to ¾ cord apple and pecan woods, or your choice

Two 5-x-4-foot pieces of wire rebar mesh

Shovel

String mop (see page 76)

6-foot table covered with plastic disposable tablecloth, for presentation

Large tray, for presentation

Cutting board

Box cutter

To Prep a Splayed Hog

Start with the hog on its back. Using a meat saw, split open the breastbone. Grab ahold of each side and pull the hog apart to separate it a bit.

(continued)

↓

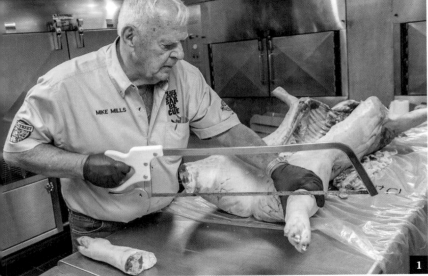

1 Remove trotters.
2 Split hog.
3 Remove fat and membranes.
4 If hog is squatted, protect loins with pieces of fat.
5 For squatted hog, insert wire mesh.

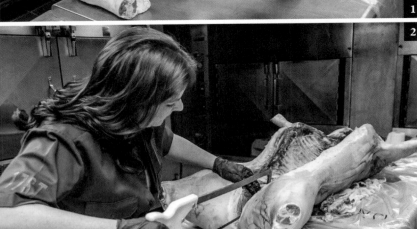

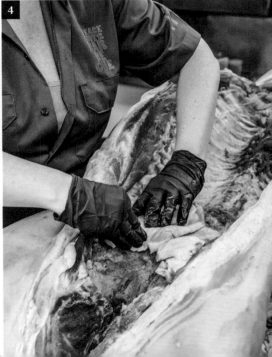

To split the backbone, start between the shoulders and use the hatchet and mallet to tap and split the hog down to the end of the backbone, about three-quarters of the way through, so the hog will open up and lay flat. Be careful—don't cut through or puncture the skin. Remove the membrane from the ribs. Trim any excess fat along the hams and shoulders. Clean off any membrane and fat from around the belly and loins. Use the fat from the belly to cover the tenderloins, right next to the backbone and in front of the hams, to help protect the delicate meat during the cook. Pry open the mouth and place a small piece of wood inside, about the size of an apple. Coat the inside of the hog with Mustard Slather and sprinkle with dry rub. Keep the hog as cold as possible until you're ready to position it on the cooker.

To Prep a Squatted Hog

Start with the hog on its back. Using a meat saw, split open the breastbone. Grab ahold of each side and pull the hog apart to separate it so that you can prep the inside. Spread the hog to expose the ribs and other meat inside. Remove the membrane from the ribs. Trim any excess fat along the hams and shoulders. Clean off any membrane and fat from around the belly and loins. Use the fat from the belly to cover the tenderloins, right next to the backbone and in front of the hams, to help protect the delicate meat during the cook. Cover the fat with a piece of foil and insert chicken wire or a folded piece of diamond mesh. This helps hold the foil in place, supports the backbone so it won't collapse, and keeps the cavity open so the smoke can get inside. Pry open the mouth and place a small piece of wood inside, about the size of an apple. Coat the inside of the hog with Mustard Slather and sprinkle with dry rub. Flip the hog over so the skin is on top. Wash the outside of the hog all over with salt water. Keep the hog as cold as possible until you're ready to position it on the pit. A squatted hog stays in that position for the entire cook.

To Cook a Splayed Hog

If using a brick pit or a cooker that requires coals shoveled underneath the hog, start a fire in the burn barrel and begin making live coals. If using an insulated cooker, see page 204.

For a brick pit or cooker that doesn't have a removable grate, center the hog on a piece of rebar mesh and put it on the pit. For a cooker with a removable grate, put the hog directly on the grate. Close the lid. Shovel a bed of coals along the perimeter of the pit or in the appropriate place for the type of cooker you're using. Check the temperature gauge. Climb to and try to maintain a steady, even temperature of 250° to 275° for the next 12 hours. Don't open the lid very often because the temperature will drop. See page 77.

North Carolina–style splayed hog on rebar mesh.

Manage the fire; see opposite. Continue to shovel coals along the perimeter of the cooker as necessary. Pile more coals near the ham and shoulder areas. Feed the burn barrel as necessary to create more live coals. This cook will take ½ to ¾ cord of wood. You can augment with charcoal if necessary.

A splayed hog starts out belly side down to absorb smoke into the meat. Flip the hog after 6 to 7 hours: Place the second piece of wire mesh on top of the hog and get several people to help clamp it down on all sides. Carefully lift the hog and flip it over, repositioning as necessary. Remove the wire mesh that is now on the top. Fill the cavity of the hog with the Hog Wash and use the mop to moisten the shoulders and hams.

Prepare the presentation area: Set up the serving table and cover it with the disposable tablecloth.

Maintain the cooker temperature at 250° to 275° until the hog reaches an internal temperature of 180° in the ham area. The ham is the largest muscle mass on the pig and if it's at 180°, the shoulder should be there, too; test the shoulder to be sure. When it temps 180°, that hog is cooked.

Pull the hog out of the cooker, still on the rebar mesh or on the removable cooking grate from the cooker, and place it on a large tray on the presentation table. Decorate the tray, using a variety of lettuce, kale, fruit, and vegetables to cover the grate or wire mesh. Replace the piece of wood in the hog's mouth with an apple or another decoration of your choice. Work quickly so you can serve the hog while it's still hot.

Serve guests strips of the belly meat and back fat, seasoned liberally with Hog Wash, dry rub, and barbecue sauce of your choice. Make sandwiches by mixing pieces of all parts of the pig—loin, shoulder, rib, belly, ham. For a special treat, hand out pieces of the belly, cheek, and red knuckle meat. Red knuckle meat is the little pocket of goodness found on the top side of the knuckle joint, at the

joint and just above. If the hog is cooked properly, you'll be able to reach in and grab that little bit of meat, which is about 2 to 3 ounces and red in hue, thus the name. If the hog is cooked at too high a heat, that meat may cook out or be dried up. Thus it's considered a delicacy. You can pull the meat from various parts of the hog and place them directly on a bun, or pull larger hunks of meat from all parts of the hog and, using a meat cleaver, chop them up on a cutting board, tossing to combine all of the parts of the hog.

MANAGING FIRE

Serious fire management is required when you're cooking a whole hog. Control the fire by opening the firebox area and cracking the lid. If you open the lid during a cooker fire, the oxygen will feed the fire and cause even more flames.

In a brick pit and on some cookers, a tented aluminum shield, drilled with holes, sits underneath the grate. As the hog cooks and the fat renders, it will drop on this shield and slide off to the ground or to the pan in the bottom of the cooker. There will be space around the perimeter of the pit, between the shield and the wall of the pit. When you're shoveling coals into the cooker, place them in that space, away from the dripping fat, so you don't start a grease fire.

To Cook a Squatted Hog

If using a brick pit or a cooker that requires coals shoveled underneath the hog, start a fire in the burn barrel and begin making live coals. If using an insulated cooker, see page 204.

For a brick pit or cooker that doesn't have a removable grate, center the hog on a piece of rebar mesh and put it on the pit. For a cooker with a removable grate, put the hog directly on the grate. Close the lid. Shovel a bed of coals along the perimeter of the pit or in the appropriate place for the type of cooker you're using. Climb to and maintain a steady, even temperature of 250° to 275° for the next 12 hours. Don't open the lid very often because the temperature will drop. See page 77.

Manage the fire; see above. Continue to shovel coals along the perimeter of the cooker as necessary. Pile more coals near the ham and shoulder areas. Feed the burn barrel as necessary to create more live coals. This will take ½ to ¾ cord of wood. You can augment with charcoal if necessary.

Prepare the presentation area: Set up the serving table and cover it with the disposable tablecloth.

Presentation for Southern Illinois–style squatted hog.

Mmaintain the cooker temperature at 250° to 275° until the hog reaches an internal temperature of 180° in the ham area. The ham is the largest muscle mass on the pig and if it's at 180°, the shoulder should be there, too; test the shoulder to be sure. When it temps 180°, that hog is cooked.

Pull the hog out of the cooker, still on the rebar mesh or on the removable cooking grate from the cooker, and place it on a large tray on the presentation table. Spray the skin with vegetable oil spray to make it glisten. Decorate the tray, using a variety of lettuce, kale, fruit, and vegetables to cover the grate or wire mesh. Replace the piece of wood in the hog's mouth with an apple or another decoration of your choice. Work quickly so you can serve the hog while it's still hot. Use a box cutter to cut three sides of a rectangular window along one side, with the top still attached so you can open and close it to preserve heat. Pull pieces of meat from all parts of the hog through that opening.

Serve guests strips of the belly meat and back fat, seasoned liberally with Hog Wash, dry rub, and barbecue sauce. Make sandwiches by mixing pieces of all parts of the pig. For special treats, hand out pieces of the belly, cheek, and red knuckle meat. Red knuckle meat is the little pocket of goodness found on the top side of the knuckle joint, at the joint and just above. If the hog is cooked properly, you'll be able to reach in and grab that little bit of meat, which is about 2 to 3 ounces and red in hue, thus the name. If the hog is cooked at too high a heat, that meat may cook out or be dried up. Thus it's considered a delicacy. You can pull the meat from various parts of the hog and place them directly on a bun, or pull larger hunks of meat from all parts of the hog and, using a meat cleaver, chop them up on a cutting board, tossing to combine all of the parts of the hog.

PICKIN' A PRETTY PIG

First, you want an upbeat pig, one that stands up tall and shows a little spirit. This isn't just my opinion: Science shows that happy pigs taste the best. Stressed pigs release adrenaline, which affects the taste of the meat. A free-roaming, pastured pig is going to be more relaxed than one raised on a feedlot. Mopey and lethargic are not good characteristics.

Second, always request a pretty face. That may sound superficial, but our pigs are on display, and we want them to look beautiful. *Southern Living* magazine named our pigs the prettiest ever, and we have a reputation to uphold. You don't want a pig with too many notches in its ear; that's how the farmer tracks its litter and age. If you see too many notches? Swipe left. (And Mike has no idea what that means!)

═Amy═

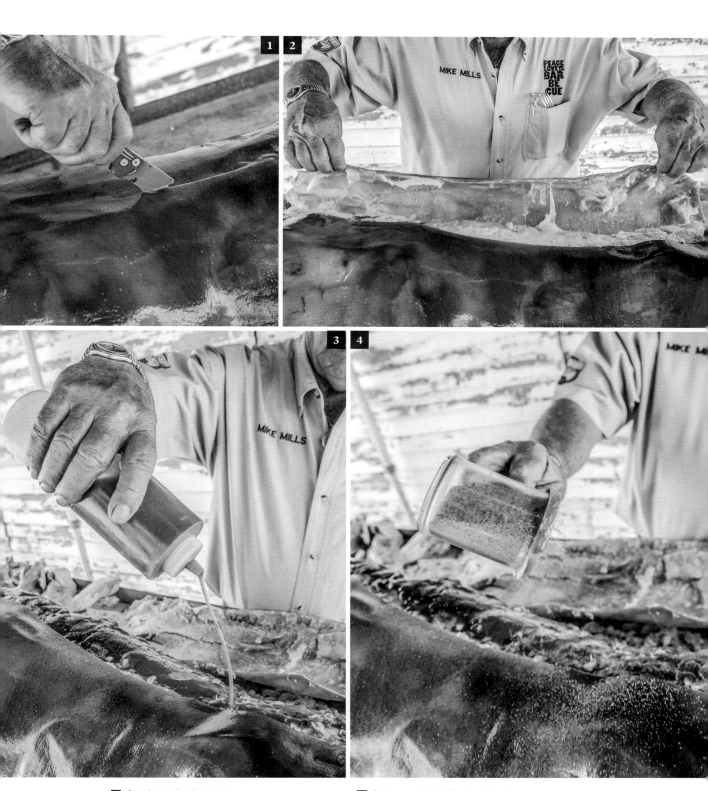

1 Slit skin with a box cutter.

2 Cut a rectangular opening in the skin.

3 Season with Hog Wash and barbecue sauce.

4 Sprinkle with dry rub.

Cooking a Whole Hog on an Insulated Cooker

Every week we cook hogs over charcoal and wood in an Ole Hickory CTO-DW. This pit, as does any other insulated cooker, turns out excellent hogs with slightly less effort because it is constructed to hold temperature for 2 to 4 hours at a time, depending on the weather that day and how often you open the door. Cooking a hog on this type of pit will require 20 to 25 pounds good-quality charcoal and 12 to 15 (12-inch) pieces of wood.

On an insulated cooker, you can cook the hog in a squatted or splayed position. If cooking the hog in a squatted position, cover the outside of the hog, including the face and ears, with heavy-duty aluminum foil. The smoke will penetrate the hog from underneath, not through the outside skin, and the foil will prevent the skin from getting too dark.

Set up the cooker for smoking: Fill the firebox with charcoal. Load a charcoal chimney one-quarter full of charcoal and light it. When the coals in the chimney are glowing, dump them on top of the charcoal already in the firebox. Alternatively, use the burner in the cooker to ignite the charcoal. Add a few pieces of wood (with no bark, so as not to create heavy smoke) on top of the charcoal.

Place the hog directly on the metal racks in the cooker and close the doors. Let the temperature climb to between 250° and 275° (see pages 84 and 77 for how to assess and monitor cooker temperature and how to determine your target). **Maintain your target temperature for the duration of the cook.** Throughout the entirety of the cook, be on the lookout for fluctuations in pit temperature; whenever it dips more than 5° below target, it's time to add a few lumps of charcoal.

Proceed with cooking the hog as directed for splayed or squatted hog.

BUILDING A BARBECUE

Until you add spice and sauce, all you have is smoked meat. Take a piece of meat and add a little Hog Wash Vinegar Splash (page 40). Taste that. It's good. Now add a little dry rub on top of that. Tastes even better. Now add a little sauce. Really good, right? Go ahead and add even a little more of what tastes good to you. Smoked meat plus dry rub plus sauce. *That's* what's called building a barbecue.

A PROPER BARBECUE SANDWICH

A proper barbecue sandwich has slaw. Our preference is for vinegar-based slaw (page 214), because the vinegar cuts through pork fat and provides the perfect balance to the richness of the pork, but buttermilk-based slaw (page 212) is good, too. We recommend skipping mayonnaise-based slaw on a sandwich as the mayonnaise, when combined with the fat from the hog, will coat the inside of your mouth.

A potato roll or a good spongy white roll or piece of bread is best—not the cheap, crumbly ones that fall apart. The bread needs to soak up the fat and sauce and hold together.

Make the sandwich with a good ratio of pulled and chopped meat with some delicious seasoned bits of bark. Make it kind of loose so you can taste all of the different textures. The beauty of the whole hog sandwich is in the mix of all of the parts of the hog—the tender shoulder, leaner ham with its fresh-cured flavor, and silky strands of belly meat, dripping with pure rendered fat. Squirt the sauce in a concentric circle, starting along the outside edge and ending in the middle, so there's a bit of sauce in each bite.

THE LANDESS MILLS SCHOOL OF BUSINESS

My brother Landess is a shrewd business-man, a real wheeler and dealer who has always known how to make money no matter where he was. Even when he was in the service during the Korean War, he had several side businesses going, so when he got home he was able to buy a panel truck and start a wholesale business selling "notions and novelties," as they called drugs and dry goods in those days.

From the time I was about ten, on weekends and days off from school, I rode with Landess on his distributing route. This was my first glimpse of working life, and it was also my introduction to entrepreneurship. I'd travel with him to all of the neighboring towns—three hours north to Springfield, an hour south to Cairo, and another thirty minutes down to Wickliffe, Kentucky—stopping at every gas station and mom-and-pop shop and grocery store along the way.

At almost every store we visited, I was given a little treat. Usually it was a lollipop or some kind of candy. We'd stop somewhere for lunch, which was a big deal because my family never dined out. My favorite was barbecue, of course, and that would always take me back to my daddy. In Cairo (pronounced KAY-roh, like the syrup), we'd go to Shemwell's or Mack's. Shemwell's had a tangy vinegar tomato sauce, while Mack's used Cairo brand, similar but a little heavier on the tomato. I always got a small bag of potato chips and a frosty glass bottle of Sunkist orange or grape soda. Sometimes I'd get root beer.

At each stop, I'd listen to Landess give his sales pitch, and I'd tag along as he brought customers out to his truck, where they would shop the racks that lined the perimeter of the vehicle and choose the items they needed. Inside the stores, as Landess stocked the shelves with shampoo, soap, health and beauty aids, aspirin, over-the-counter medicines, and combs, he explained to me how he had to rotate the merchandise, and how much the merchandise cost and how much he could make. I learned the fundamentals of how business worked—things I could only later put names to, like profit margins and competitive pricing.

I also learned that civility and respect, honor and trust were essential. A guy might say, "I'm running a little low on funds and I need this, but I can't pay you until the next visit." And those people would pay when we came back through weeks later—mostly. Over time, observing these dealings taught me that this is how business is conducted. Some people you trust, a few you don't. Some people got credit, some didn't.

Observing that business owners seemed to be more prosperous and in charge than other types of workers we encountered, I resolved to have a business of my own. And to this day, I marvel at Landess's acumen as I watch him, still at it, wheeling and dealing in his office at The Warehouse at 17th Street.

═Mike═

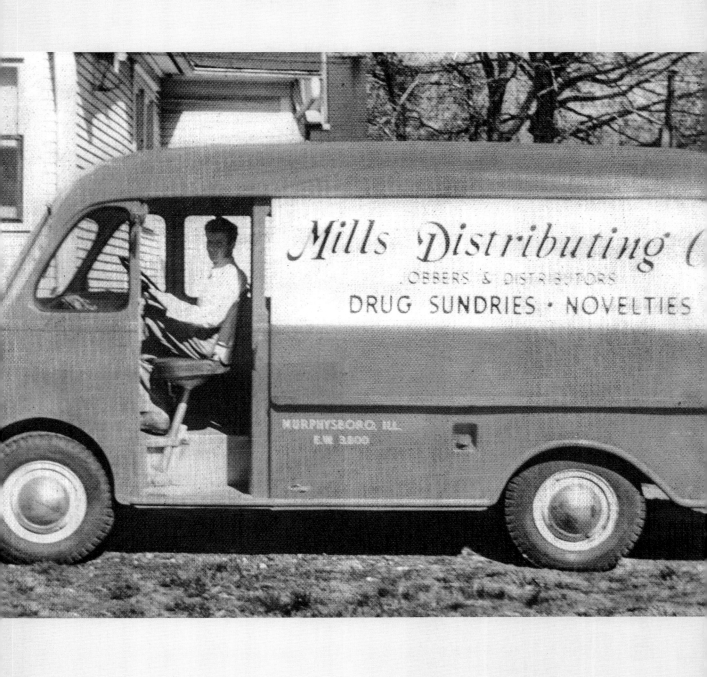

THE DISCIPLES

GREAT BARBECUE SIDE DISHES

OUR REPUTATION for side dishes that shine was established decades before 17th Street was even a glimmer in Mike's eye. Going back at least a couple of generations, ours has long been a family of cooks, with various members bringing their very own painstakingly perfected versions of classic side dishes to family gatherings and church potlucks.

We've compiled our family recipes into a compendium of accompaniments, all classics, all refined in ways that elevate standards to standouts. Whether it's a particular spice, a tweaked technique, a secret ingredient, or an unexpected element that imparts to each dish a certain something special, these are the sides that have earned a place on our table.

HOME-STYLE POTATO SALAD

MAKES 6 TO 8 SERVINGS

Every family ought to have a good potato salad recipe. This is ours. The potatoes must be perfectly cooked—not too hard or too mushy. Make this well in advance—the flavors need time to blend, and it should be served well chilled.

1½ pounds small red-skinned potatoes, scrubbed

Kosher salt

½ cup finely chopped onion

3 large eggs, hard cooked, peeled, and chopped

1½ tablespoons celery seeds

¾ cup mayonnaise (we use Hellmann's)

½ cup sour cream

¼ cup Buttermilk Ranch (page 57)

1 tablespoon pickle juice or dill pickle relish

½ teaspoon ground white pepper

½ teaspoon dry mustard (we use Colman's)

½ teaspoon sugar

Pure Magic dry rub (page 29) or sweet Hungarian paprika, or 1 tablespoon finely chopped scallion tops or fresh chives, for garnish

Put the potatoes in a large pot of salted water. Bring to a boil and cook for about 40 minutes, or just until tender. Test the potatoes by sliding the blade of a sharp knife into a potato. When it slides out clean, the potatoes are done. Don't overcook them or you'll end up with mashed potato salad.

Drain the potatoes in a large colander. When they are cool enough to handle, halve each potato, then stand them on the cut ends and slice into ¼-inch half-moons, leaving the skins on. Transfer the still-warm potatoes to a large bowl and toss them with the onion, eggs, and celery seeds.

In a separate bowl, make a dressing by mixing the mayonnaise, sour cream, Buttermilk Ranch, pickle juice, 1 teaspoon salt, the white pepper, mustard, and sugar.

Pour the dressing over the potatoes and mix gently with clean hands until the potatoes are well coated. Sprinkle the top lightly with Pure Magic or paprika or garnish with the scallions or chives if desired. Cover and refrigerate for 4 to 6 hours before serving.

BUTTERMILK-SPIKED COLE SLAW

MAKES 8 TO 10 SERVINGS

Mayonnaise-based dressing can coat your mouth, whereas buttermilk and a bit of sugar keep this classic slaw creamy while providing just the right amount of tangy sweetness. Use the slaw as a topping for pulled pork sandwiches and as a side dish.

1 cup full-fat buttermilk

⅔ cup sugar

¼ cup rice vinegar

1 tablespoon fresh lemon juice

1 teaspoon kosher salt

¼ teaspoon ground white pepper

1 medium green cabbage

¼ small purple cabbage

1 carrot, peeled and shredded

2 tablespoons minced onion

In a large bowl, combine the buttermilk, sugar, vinegar, lemon juice, salt, and pepper and stir until smooth. Using a very large sharp knife, slice the cabbages into ¼-inch-thick slices. Lay the slices flat and finely chop them, first sideways, then up and down. You should have about 6½ cups green cabbage and ½ cup purple. Add the cabbage, along with the carrot and onion, to the buttermilk mixture and toss until well coated. Cover and refrigerate for several hours, until chilled. The slaw keeps, refrigerated, for 3 days.

TANGY VINEGAR COLE SLAW

MAKES 8 TO 10 SERVINGS

This simple vinegar-based cole slaw is our number one side dish. It's a hallowed tradition on a barbecue sandwich—the tart, crunchy cabbage goes perfectly with the smoky flavor of the meat, and the vinegar helps cut through the pork fat. Leftovers can be parlayed into Soul Rolls (page 59) or Barbecue Parfaits (page 133).

1 medium green cabbage

¼ small purple cabbage

1 carrot, peeled and shredded

DRESSING

2 cups apple cider vinegar

2 cups sugar

½ cup chopped onion

¼ cup chopped green pepper

1¼ tablespoons canola oil or other mild vegetable oil

1½ teaspoons celery seeds

1½ teaspoons granulated garlic

1 teaspoon dry mustard (we use Colman's)

½ teaspoon kosher salt

½ teaspoon freshly ground black pepper

Using a large sharp knife, slice the cabbages into ¼-inch-thick slices. Lay the slices flat and finely chop them, first sideways, then up and down. You should have about 5 cups green cabbage and 1 cup purple. Toss the green and purple cabbages and the carrot in a large bowl.

For the dressing: In another bowl, mix the vinegar, sugar, onion, green pepper, oil, celery seeds, garlic, dry mustard, salt, and pepper, stirring until the sugar is dissolved.

With a measuring cup, transfer half of the dressing to the bowl with the cabbage and carrots. Toss with clean hands or a large spatula to combine. Keep adding the dressing, ¼ cup at a time, being careful not to drench the cabbage. You may not need all of the dressing; any leftover can be saved in a covered container in the refrigerator for up to 5 days and used as a dressing for salad or to marinate vegetables.

Cover and refrigerate for several hours, until chilled. The slaw keeps, refrigerated, for 5 days.

CHOW

MAKES 1 QUART

In some parts of the South people call this condiment "chow chow"; here in Southern Illinois, we simply call it "chow." We use it as a topping for sliced barbecue sandwiches.

¼ cup chopped green pepper

¼ cup chopped onion

2 cups apple cider vinegar

½ medium green cabbage

⅛ small purple cabbage

1 carrot, peeled

2 cups sugar

1 tablespoon vegetable oil

1 tablespoon kosher salt

2 tablespoons freshly ground black pepper

1½ teaspoons dry mustard (we use Colman's)

1½ teaspoons hot sauce (we use Frank's RedHot)

1 teaspoon celery seeds

½ teaspoon granulated garlic

Pulse the green pepper, onion, and 2 tablespoons of the apple cider vinegar in a blender or food processor until finely chopped, but not mushy. Finely chop the green and purple cabbages and carrot by hand, or pulse them separately in the food processor. Combine the green pepper and onion mixture, cabbages, and carrot in a large bowl and stir together.

In a saucepan, combine the remaining apple cider vinegar with the sugar, oil, salt, pepper, mustard, hot sauce, celery seeds, and garlic. Bring to a boil, whisking constantly, until the sugar is dissolved and the mixture begins to bubble.

Pour the vinegar mixture over the vegetables and stir to combine. Transfer to glass jars or a large airtight container. Cover and refrigerate for up to 1 month. Serve cold, as a condiment.

BIG BOWL OF SUMMER CORN SALAD

MAKES 6 TO 8 SERVINGS

We revel in the bounty of the corn crop in Southern Illinois, and this fresh, bright corn salad filled with vegetables is a healthy crowd pleaser. Fresh lima beans are difficult to find, but use them if they're available.

2 tablespoons extra virgin olive oil

½ cup chopped red onion

½ small orange pepper, chopped

½ small red pepper, chopped

½ small yellow pepper, chopped

2 tablespoons unsalted butter

Kernels sliced from 6 ears fresh corn (3 to 4 cups)

½ cup shelled baby lima beans (fresh or frozen)

1 teaspoon kosher salt

1 teaspoon freshly ground black pepper

2 tablespoons chopped fresh basil

2 tablespoons chopped fresh chives

2 tablespoons chopped fresh flat-leaf parsley

Heat the olive oil in a medium saucepan and add the onion. Cook, stirring, for several minutes, until the onion begins to soften. Add the peppers and cook, stirring, for 3 to 4 minutes, until slightly tender. Add the butter. When the butter is melted, stir in the corn, lima beans, salt, and pepper. Cook, stirring constantly, for 3 to 4 minutes, just until warmed through. Season to taste with salt and pepper. Remove from the heat and gently stir in the basil, chives, and parsley. Taste and adjust the seasoning as needed. Serve hot or cold. It's best served the same day.

BRISKET-SEASONED COLLARDS

MAKES 8 TO 10 SERVINGS

John Delpha of Rosebud American Kitchen & Bar in Somerville, Massachusetts, is the brains behind this dish, and he was kind enough to share the recipe, to which we've added our own twists. John's secret is that he uses duck fat, left over from the duck confit that he makes in his restaurant. You can buy duck fat at specialty grocery stores, or just use another type of fat. We're partial to brisket fat, and this is another use for the leftover pieces of seasoned fat and meat from brisket, pastrami, pork butts, or pork shoulder. (The rub and smoke season the fat as it renders.) Put all of those leftovers in the freezer, well wrapped in plastic and in a freezer bag. Then thaw, chop, and sauté when you're ready to use them. You can also use rendered chicken or pork fat with delicious results.

1½ cups diced brisket (page 110) or pastrami (page 118) trimmings, fat and meat combined; or ¼ pound smoked bacon, cut into ¼-inch cubes, plus 2 tablespoons pork, brisket, or duck fat

½ cup thinly sliced onion

3 bunches collards (3 pounds), washed thoroughly, stems removed, leaves coarsely chopped

¼ cup packed light brown sugar

2 tablespoons pure cane syrup (see page 19) or molasses

Kosher salt and freshly ground black pepper

¼ cup apple cider vinegar, plus more to taste

½ teaspoon red pepper flakes

Cook the trimmings or bacon in a large heavy-bottom pot over medium heat to render the fat and get the trimmings or bacon brown and crispy. Add the onion and cook, stirring frequently, until softened, about 5 minutes. Add the collards, brown sugar, cane syrup, and a pinch of salt and pepper and stir to combine.

Continue cooking over medium-low heat until the collards release their juices and the liquid has almost completely evaporated, about 30 minutes. Add the vinegar, red pepper flakes, and 1 quart water. Raise the heat to medium-high. Continue cooking, uncovered, stirring occasionally, until the collards are tender, about 1 hour. There should be about 1 cup of potlikker (the collards' juices) when finished. Season to taste with additional salt, pepper, and a touch more vinegar.

CHARRED GARDEN VEGETABLES

Cooking vegetables over fire releases their natural sugars and deepens their flavors. We like them simply seasoned with salt and pepper, but dry rub works well, too.

Broccolini, separated into branches and trimmed

Asparagus, trimmed

Carrots, trimmed and scrubbed

Leeks, trimmed

Beets, trimmed and peeled

Red and yellow peppers

Red onion, trimmed and peeled

Olive oil

Kosher salt and freshly ground black pepper

Fresh thyme or other fresh herbs, for garnish

3 pounds lump charcoal

Wash the vegetables and lay the broccolini and asparagus out on paper towels. Cut the carrots and leeks in half lengthwise, and quarter the beets, peppers, and onion. Prepare a large bowl of ice water and bring a large pot of salted water to a boil.

Working with one vegetable at a time, boil the carrots, leeks, and beets for 3 to 5 minutes. Transfer to the ice water for about 1 minute. Pat dry with paper towels. (Cook and chill the beets last, so they don't turn the other vegetables pink.)

Combine all the vegetables in a large bowl or on a baking sheet. Drizzle with olive oil, season well with salt and pepper, and toss to coat.

Set up the cooker for direct cooking: Open the top and bottom vents. Pile 2 pounds of the charcoal in the bottom. Load a charcoal chimney one-quarter full of charcoal and light it. When the coals in the chimney are glowing, dump them on top of the pile already in the cooker and close the lid. Adjust the vents as necessary to establish a steady temperature between 350° to 375° for direct grilling (see pages 84 and 77 for how to best assess and monitor cooker temperature, and how to determine your target temperature). Open the cooker and spread the vegetables evenly over the grate and cook for 3 to 4 minutes, or until the edges begin to char. Flip and cook for 3 to 4 minutes on the other side, or until the peppers, broccolini, asparagus, and onion are charred at the edges and slightly soft (pull individual pieces off as they reach this point). Transfer to a large serving platter. The beets, carrots, and leeks will take a few minutes longer; don't let them get too soft.

Garnish the platter with herb sprigs. Serve the vegetables hot or at room temperature. Leftovers can be refrigerated and eaten cold, or chopped for salads.

MIKE'S FROM-SCRATCH BAKED BEANS

These are not your average baked beans. Using four different varieties and scratch-cooking them from dried makes for a deliciously complex combination of flavors and textures, while a mix of savory spices, brown sugar, and honey adds tang and sweetness. Bear in mind that the dried beans will need time to soak. And be selective about what you buy: Take a pass on bagged beans that contain a lot of shriveled or broken bits, and consider giving specialty beans a try. We've found there really is a difference when you use quality beans straight from a grower, such as Rancho Gordo (see Resources, page 321).

The recipe calls for a ham hock or bacon, but you can season this dish with all kinds of leftover cooked meat—strips of bacon, bits of fatty brisket, pulled pork, or a few cooked ribs. Finally, if you want a smaller yield, you can freeze half the batch before baking. Leftovers also freeze well.

1 cup dried great Northern beans

½ cup dried small red beans

½ cup dried light red kidney beans

½ cup dried baby lima beans

½ cup dried large lima beans

1 small meaty ham hock or 3 to 4 strips of bacon; or leftover cooked and smoked meat such as fatty bits of brisket, pulled pork, or a few ribs

1½ teaspoons kosher salt

2 cups ketchup (made with cane sugar, such as Red Gold or Hunt's)

1 large onion, diced

1 green bell pepper, diced

1½ cups light brown sugar

½ cup local honey

1½ tablespoons Pure Magic dry rub (page 29) or your choice

1 tablespoon prepared yellow mustard

1½ teaspoons dry mustard (we use Colman's)

Combine the beans in a large colander and rinse well, picking through and discarding any debris as well as broken, darkened, or otherwise old-looking beans. Transfer the beans to a stockpot and add enough cold water to cover by several inches. Skim off and discard any floating beans.

Transfer the pot to the refrigerator and soak the beans for 4 to 8 hours, depending on how fresh they are.

(continued)

↓

Drain and rinse the beans. Rinse out the pot. Return the beans to the pot and add the ham hock and enough water to cover by several inches. Bring the mixture to a boil, then lower the heat and simmer, uncovered, for 1 hour, skimming off any foam.

Check the beans for tenderness: When you can bite through one of them but it's not yet tender to the center, they are about three-quarters of the way cooked and it is time to salt them. (Salting sooner greatly prolongs cook time; salting later means the salt doesn't penetrate the beans, so you get salty broth and bland beans.) Add the salt and 1 cup of the ketchup and simmer the beans for another 30 minutes, or until tender at the center but not soft.

Ladle out and reserve 1½ cups of the cooking broth. Drain the beans, transfer them to a large bowl, and set aside to cool to room temperature.

Preheat the oven to 350°, with a rack in the center.

In a medium bowl, combine the remaining 1 cup ketchup with the onion, bell pepper, brown sugar, honey, dry rub, prepared mustard, dry mustard, and the reserved bean broth. Add to the beans, and using your hands or a large wooden spoon, gently mix, taking care to keep the skins of the beans intact.

Transfer the beans to a 13-x-9-inch baking dish. Bake for about 1 hour, until bubbling. Alternatively, transfer half of the beans to an 8-inch-square baking pan and bake until bubbling (about 45 minutes). Freeze the remainder in a freezer bag for up to 3 months; thaw in the refrigerator before baking.

CHICKEN AND DUMPLINGS

MAKES 6 TO 8 SERVINGS AS A MEAL, 8 TO 10 SIDE SERVINGS

A steaming tureen of chicken and dumplings graced the table at many Sunday suppers when I was growing up. This is one recipe I didn't learn from my mom before she passed away, so Judith Anne Tweedy, one of my mom's dear friends, took me under her wing and taught me her delicious version. Mike says this dish is best when made with a big, old hen—a 6- to 8-pounder (good luck finding one). —Amy

One 5- to 6-pound chicken

1 tablespoon kosher salt, plus more to taste

1 tablespoon coarsely ground black pepper, plus more to taste

1 teaspoon granulated garlic

6 tablespoons (¾ stick) unsalted butter

1 medium onion, diced

2 medium celery stalks, diced

5 bay leaves

2 carrots, chopped

1 tablespoon chicken base (such as Better Than Bouillon)

¼ cup all-purpose flour

2 tablespoons chopped fresh flat-leaf parsley

DUMPLINGS

3 cups all-purpose flour (we use King Arthur), plus more for dusting

1½ teaspoons baking powder

1 teaspoon kosher salt

2 large eggs

½ cup vegetable oil

Kosher salt and coarsely ground black pepper

Remove the packet of innards from the cavity of the chicken. Rinse and reserve the heart, gizzards, and neck; discard the liver. Mix the salt, pepper, and granulated garlic in a small bowl. Sprinkle all over the chicken and pat to help it adhere.

Melt 2 tablespoons of the butter in a large, deep stockpot over medium-high heat and cook the onion and celery for 5 to 6 minutes, until they are translucent and there are lots of nice brown bits on the bottom of the pan. Remove and reserve.

Put the chicken in the pot, breast down. Throw in the heart, gizzards, and neck as well. Cook on medium-high for about 5 minutes, until the chicken begins to brown. Add enough cold water to cover the chicken by 1 inch. Add the bay leaves, carrots, reserved sautéed vegetables, and the chicken base. Turn the heat to high, bring to a boil, then lower the heat to a simmer, cover, and cook for about 1 hour, until a thigh reaches 165° on an instant-read thermometer. Stick a large wooden spoon down into the cavity of the chicken and carefully lift the chicken out of the pot. Let the broth drain back into the pot. Put the chicken on a rimmed baking sheet to cool. Fish out the heart, gizzards, and neck; add to the baking sheet with the chicken. Remove and discard the bay leaves.

(continued)

↓

Scoop out ¾ cup of the broth for the dumplings and set it aside to cool in the refrigerator. Pour another cup of the broth into a small bowl and whisk in the flour to make a slurry. Set aside.

Taste the remaining broth and season with more salt and pepper as needed. Add the remaining 4 tablespoons butter. Keep the broth on a low simmer while you're making the dumplings and deboning the chicken.

When the chicken is cool enough to handle, remove and discard the skin. Separate the meat from the bones and discard the bones. Cut the meat into 2- to 3-inch pieces and return to the baking sheet. Chop up the heart and gizzards and pull any meat from the neck; add to the chicken. Discard the neck bone. Loosely cover and set aside.

For the dumplings: Line a baking sheet with parchment paper. Generously dust a clean work surface with flour. Mix together the flour, baking powder, and salt in a large bowl. In a separate bowl, beat the eggs with a fork, then beat in the oil and the reserved ¾ cup broth. Make a well in the dry ingredients and pour in the egg mixture. Use your fingers to toss the flour and liquid together, just enough to combine. Knead the dough in the bowl with your hands, until it's evenly mixed. Turn it out onto the work surface and divide in half. Roll each half out to a ⅛-inch thickness. Slice the dough diagonally into 2-inch-wide strips, then slice in the opposite direction to form diamonds 2 to 3 inches long. Dust the dumplings with flour, separate, and carefully transfer to the baking sheet.

Add 1 quart water to the simmering broth, stir to combine, and taste and adjust the salt and pepper again. Bring to a boil. Drop the dumplings one by one into the boiling broth, stirring gently as you add them. Reduce the heat and simmer until the dumplings are tender, about 10 minutes, occasionally stirring gently to prevent clumping. Add a bit of the reserved flour-broth slurry and stir until the broth thickens as desired. It should be a pale golden color.

Gently stir in the chicken and continue to simmer until heated through. Season to taste with additional salt and pepper. Stir in the parsley just before serving.

CHEESY POTATOES

MAKES 12 TO 15 SERVINGS

Creamy, cheesy potatoes are pure comfort food and a staple at any family gathering. This version is one of our most requested dishes for parties we cater and for gatherings after funerals. You may want to make a double batch and pop one in the freezer for future use.

1 teaspoon butter, softened

2 cups whole milk

¼ medium onion

2 garlic cloves, peeled and left whole

3 sprigs fresh thyme

3 pounds potatoes, coarsely shredded

2 teaspoons kosher salt

1 tablespoon coarsely ground black pepper

2 tablespoons all-purpose flour

2 cups sour cream, at room temperature

2½ cups (about 10 ounces) grated cheddar cheese

½ cup cornflake crumbs

½ cup chopped Lacquered Bacon (page 50) or cooked bacon (optional)

2 teaspoons finely chopped fresh flat-leaf parsley

Preheat the oven to 400°, with a rack in the center. Grease a 13-x-9-inch baking dish or large casserole with the butter.

In a medium saucepan over medium-low heat, combine the milk, onion, garlic, and thyme and heat just until steaming. Take the pan off the heat, cover, and let steep for about 10 minutes.

Put the potatoes in the baking dish and season with the salt and pepper, tossing to mix.

Pour the milk mixture through a strainer into a mixing bowl. Gradually whisk in the flour, mixing very thoroughly. Whisk in the sour cream. Pour the mixture over the potatoes. Cover the dish with foil, carefully slide it into the oven, and bake for 1 to 1½ hours or until the potatoes are tender (use a small sharp knife to check potatoes in various parts of the dish; the tip of the knife should slide in easily), rotating the dish halfway through the cooking time.

Sprinkle the cheese all over the top of the potatoes. Top with a thin, even layer of the crumbs and scatter on the chopped bacon, if desired, and the parsley. Bake 15 to 30 minutes longer, or until the top is a deep golden brown. Serve hot.

REAL-DEAL MAC AND CHEESE

MAKES ABOUT 12 SERVINGS

This is what mac and cheese in the box wishes it could be. Don't turn your nose up at the Velveeta—that's what makes the texture ultra creamy. Cheddar and Parmesan bring a sharp tang, and the interplay of cheeses, seasonings, and panko topping take the whole situation over the top. Cooking the pasta to al dente is important—nothing is worse than soggy macaroni.

8 tablespoons (1 stick) unsalted butter, plus more for the pan

Kosher salt

1 pound elbow macaroni

6 tablespoons all-purpose flour

4 cups whole milk

¾ cup heavy cream

1½ tablespoons dry mustard

½ teaspoon ground white pepper

¼ teaspoon freshly grated nutmeg

2½ cups (10 ounces) hand-grated extra-sharp cheddar cheese

8 ounces (one half of a 1-pound block) Velveeta cheese, cut into 1-inch cubes

About ½ cup finely grated Parmesan cheese

¼ cup panko bread crumbs

Preheat the oven to 400°, with a rack in the center. Butter a 13-x-9-inch baking dish. Line a baking sheet with parchment paper. Bring a large pot of salted water to boil.

Add the macaroni to the boiling water and cook until al dente. Drain and set aside.

Melt the butter in a large saucepan over medium heat. Add the flour a little at a time, whisking to incorporate. Cook the roux, stirring constantly with a wooden spoon, for about 4 minutes, or until it is bubbly and starting to brown. Gradually pour in the milk and cream, whisking constantly to incorporate. Raise the heat to medium-high and bring the sauce to a low boil, continuing to whisk constantly. Reduce to a simmer, and cook, whisking occasionally, until the sauce is thick and coats the back of the wooden spoon.

Stir in 2 teaspoons salt and the mustard, pepper, and nutmeg. Stir in 2 cups of the cheddar and the Velveeta cubes, a cup at a time, completely melting each addition before adding more. Take the pan off the heat.

Add the macaroni to the cheese sauce and stir to coat. Scrape into the baking dish and place on the baking sheet. Sprinkle the remaining ½ cup cheddar, the Parmesan, and the bread crumbs evenly over the top. Bake until golden brown and bubbling, 20 to 25 minutes. Serve hot.

SAVORY CORNBREAD PUDDING

MAKES ONE 8-INCH PAN

Cooking this ultra moist cornbread in a cast-iron skillet makes the edges crispy while the center is pudding-like. It crumbles on the plate in the most delicious way. Make it with lard if you possibly can, as it makes the texture moist and delicate like nothing else. The quality of cornmeal also makes a difference in the texture and taste; experiment with varieties of local, organic cornmeal if available. If you use self-rising cornmeal, omit the baking powder.

1½ cups medium or coarse grind cornmeal, yellow or white

2 tablespoons baking powder

3 large eggs

½ cup plus 1 heaping tablespoon lard, softened, or ½ cup vegetable oil plus 1 heaping tablespoon unsalted butter

One 14.75-ounce can creamed corn

1 cup sour cream

1 teaspoon kosher salt

Place an 8-inch cast-iron skillet on a rack in the center of the oven and preheat the oven to 375°.

In a small bowl, sift together the cornmeal and baking powder. Set aside.

Thoroughly mix the eggs and ½ cup of the lard in a medium bowl. Add the creamed corn, sour cream, and salt, mixing well. Fold in the cornmeal mixture just enough to barely combine.

Carefully take the hot skillet from the oven and add the remaining tablespoon of lard. Swirl to generously coat the bottom and sides of the pan. (The fat will pool a bit in the bottom of the pan, and that is a good thing.) Pour the batter into the skillet. Place the skillet in the oven, and place a baking sheet or piece of aluminum foil on the rack below the pan to capture any overflow.

Bake for 20 minutes, or until the pudding is puffed and golden, browned at the edges, and a tester inserted in the center comes out with a few moist crumbs attached. Serve warm.

THE BEST
BUTTERMILK BISCUITS

MAKES TWELVE 2½-INCH BISCUITS

Baking flaky, tender biscuits is really all about the technique and a few simple high-quality ingredients. A lesson from Nashville pastry chef Lisa Donovan helped us take our biscuits to a whole new level: Work with a cold bowl and cold dry ingredients. Using full-fat buttermilk is important, and if you have a local dairy that sells buttermilk, that will be the best. (We haul Cruze Farm buttermilk back from Nashville whenever we visit.) Lift the biscuit cutter straight up when you're cutting the dough; twisting the cutter seals the edges and prevents the biscuits from rising properly. Biscuits need something to rise up against, so crowd them in a skillet or baking pan so that they're touching each other and the edge of the skillet or pan—which must be preheated to scorching hot.

Lisa swears by King Arthur flour, which opposes the popular Southern commandment of insisting upon White Lily. We made dozens of batches using each type of flour, and it's really a matter of personal preference. King Arthur flour is unbleached, so it gives the biscuits more substantial flavor. A biscuit made with White Lily flour is softer. Both are flaky and delicious, so the choice is yours.

Serve instead of bread or rolls at supper with Sweet Strawberry Butter (page 242) or Top-Shelf Bourbon Butter (page 241).

2 cups all-purpose flour (King Arthur or White Lily), plus more for rolling

1½ teaspoons baking powder

½ teaspoon baking soda

1½ teaspoons kosher salt

6 tablespoons (¾ stick) unsalted butter, cut into small pieces and chilled, plus 1 tablespoon for the skillet and 1 tablespoon, melted, for brushing

½ to ¾ cup full-fat buttermilk

Set a 10-inch cast-iron skillet on a rack in the center of the oven and preheat the oven to 475°.

In a large, chilled mixing bowl, whisk together the flour with the baking powder, baking soda, and salt. Drop in the butter and, using a pastry cutter, cut it into the flour just until the mixture resembles coarse meal. Work quickly so the dough remains as chilled as possible. Add ½ cup of buttermilk and circle the bowl with a spatula to toss and moisten the flour. Add more buttermilk as necessary, just

enough for the mixture to begin to gather into a dough but not form a single mass. Chill the dough in the refrigerator for about 10 minutes.

Lightly flour the work surface and a rolling pin. Turn the dough out onto the work surface and gather the clumps together, folding the dough over on itself a few times. Form the dough into a disk and roll it out to a 12-inch circle that's about 1 inch thick. Using a 2½-inch biscuit cutter, cut out the biscuits as close together as possible. Gather the scraps, re-roll, and cut as needed to form 12 biscuits.

Carefully take the skillet out of the oven and add 1 tablespoon butter. Let it melt; swirl to coat the bottom. Arrange 9 of the biscuits against the edge of the skillet in a tight ring, then squeeze the remaining 3 biscuits into the center of the ring.

Bake for 4 to 6 minutes, then rotate the pan and brush the tops of the biscuits with the melted butter. Bake for 2 to 4 more minutes, until the biscuits are golden. Serve immediately.

HERB AND GARLIC BUTTER

MAKES 1 CUP

Press this butter into a ramekin or roll it into a log, chill, and cut into slices to top a steak (page 123). Bring to room temperature for spreading on biscuits or buttering ears of corn, baked potatoes, or vegetables.

2 cups packed fresh herb leaves of your choice (we use flat-leaf parsley, chives, and basil)

½ small garlic clove

8 tablespoons (1 stick) unsalted butter, softened

½ teaspoon finely grated lemon zest

1 teaspoon fresh lemon juice

⅛ to ¼ teaspoon kosher salt

⅛ to ¼ teaspoon coarsely ground black pepper

Pulse the herbs and garlic in a food processor until finely chopped. Add the butter, lemon zest, and lemon juice and process until smooth. Season with salt and pepper to taste and pulse to combine. Scrape the butter into a ramekin and cover with plastic wrap, or scrape onto a sheet of parchment paper and form into a cylinder about 2 inches in diameter. Roll the paper to cover it and twist the ends. Wrap in foil to keep airtight, and refrigerate or freeze. The butter keeps in the refrigerator for up to 1 week or in the freezer for up to 1 month.

Clockwise: Top-Shelf Bourbon Butter; Herb and Garlic Butter; Sweet Strawberry Butter

TOP-SHELF BOURBON BUTTER

MAKES ABOUT ½ CUP

You'll come up with a dozen uses for this sweet and savory butter, spiked with a shot of your best bourbon. Press the butter into a ramekin or small bowl and bring to room temperature for spreading on a biscuit or roll, or form a log and chill it if you're going to slice off pieces to top pork chops (page 104).

8 tablespoons (1 stick) unsalted butter, softened

1 tablespoon bourbon (we use Willett)

1 tablespoon pure maple syrup or cane syrup (see page 19)

1 teaspoon light brown sugar

⅛ to ¼ teaspoon kosher salt

Combine the butter, bourbon, maple syrup, brown sugar, and ⅛ teaspoon of the salt in a small bowl. Using a fork, mash until well combined. Alternatively, pulse the ingredients together in a food processor. Taste and season with additional salt as needed. Scrape the butter into a ramekin and cover with plastic wrap. Alternatively, scrape the butter onto a sheet of parchment paper and form into a log about 2 inches in diameter, rolling the parchment paper to cover the log and twisting the ends of the paper to close. Wrap in foil to keep airtight. Chill in the refrigerator or freeze.

Bring the butter to room temperature before spreading. Keep the log slightly chilled for slicing. The butter keeps in the refrigerator for up to 2 weeks or in the freezer for up to 1 month.

SWEET STRAWBERRY BUTTER

MAKES 1 CUP

Make this butter in the late spring, at the height of the season to take advantage of the full fruity flavor of fresh strawberries. If you're making it out of season, taste the berries and make sure they have flavor and aren't weak or watery. Spread on biscuits, rolls, or pancakes.

8 tablespoons (1 stick) unsalted butter, softened

1 tablespoon powdered sugar

⅛ teaspoon kosher salt

½ cup hulled and coarsely chopped fresh strawberries

With an electric mixer, beat the butter, powdered sugar, and salt until light, about 1 minute. Add the strawberries and beat until just combined. The berries should still be chunky. Alternatively, pulse all the ingredients in a food processor.

Scrape the butter into a ramekin and cover with plastic wrap. Alternatively, scrape the butter onto a sheet of parchment paper and form into a log about 2 inches in diameter. Roll the parchment paper to cover it and twist the ends. Wrap in foil to keep airtight. Chill in the refrigerator or freeze.

Bring to room temperature before using. The butter keeps in the refrigerator for up to 1 week, or in the freezer for up to 1 month.

GRILLED FRUIT

A quick spin on the grill brings out the natural sweetness and adds a bit of smoky char to almost any fruit. We like to grill fruit to use in cocktails or add to ice cream, and it's also the perfect accompaniment to meat. Of course, it's delicious on its own.

Pineapple	Grapefruit	Plums
Light brown sugar	Oranges	
Peaches	Lemons	3 pounds good-quality lump charcoal
Vegetable oil	Demerara sugar	

Cut the pineapple into wedges or spears. Press the cut sides into the brown sugar. Cut the peaches in half, remove the pits, and lightly oil the peach halves. Cut the citrus fruits in half and press the cut sides into the Demerara sugar. Lightly brush oil onto the plums.

Set up the cooker for direct cooking: Open the top and bottom vents. Pile 2 pounds of the charcoal in the bottom. Load a charcoal chimney one-quarter full of charcoal and light it. When the coals in the chimney are glowing, dump them on top of the pile already in the cooker and close the lid. Adjust the vents as necessary to establish a steady temperature between 350° to 375° for direct grilling (see pages 84 and 77 for how to best assess and monitor cooker temperature, and how to determine your target temperature). Open the cooker and spread the fruits evenly over the charcoal, cut side down, and cook for 3 to 4 minutes, or until they soften and are nicely marked. Pull the fruits off the cooker and arrange on a large serving tray.

Serve immediately or at room temperature. The grapefruit, oranges, and lemons can also be juiced for cocktails (page 251).

FAMILY VALUES

I jokingly call myself a barbecue heiress, but the Mills legacy is so much more than a business. My brother, cousins, and I were schooled in the value of a job well done from a very early age. Most of us received intensive instruction at the Mama Faye School of Proper Lawn Mowing, and we all worked after school and on weekends for our uncles as well as in our parents' own businesses.

In middle school and high school, I was employed in Daddy's dental lab after school, typing up invoices on a typewriter I borrowed from my Uncle John's dental practice downstairs. I was thrilled when Uncle Landess gave me a second job as a sales clerk a few days a week at Mills Distributing Company. At that time, Daddy also owned the Corner Tavern, but I was too young and too female to work there.

Uncle Landess's store was a catalog showroom, where you could buy almost anything you needed, from household goods, gifts, and small appliances to photography and camping equipment. People registered there for their weddings, and he also sold fine jewelry.

One day, Daddy called Mills Distributing and asked to speak to me. "She's already gone," Uncle Landess said. "They all bolt out of here at the stroke of five o'clock." That story was relayed back to me in such a way that I got the message loud and clear. From then on out, I busied myself wiping counters and vacuuming right up until closing time, and I made sure I was the last to leave.

What was handed down, in addition to entrepreneurial spirit, was fortitude and grit. When the going got tough and I had to provide for two children, I figured out a way to make extra money—doing graphic design work, freelance copywriting, and running a consulting company that had me traveling around the country, all while maintaining a full-time job.

Fast-forward twenty years, and it was high time my son, Woody, got a real taste of actual hard work. At thirteen, he had little tortoise shell glasses and was dressed like a miniature figure from *The Official Preppy Handbook*. His passions were reading and architecture.

After his first day of working the 17th Street trailer at the Illinois State Fair, his grandfather called with a report:

"We were in the food trailer, setting up, and Woody was sitting on a five-gallon bucket. 'Grampy Mike,' he asked me, 'what is our break schedule?'"

"Break schedule? Break schedule? When we have no line, you're on break. When we have a line, you're off break!"

Woody called a few days later. "I'll have you know I haven't eaten lunch since I got here," he told me. "We have no lunch hour!"

Stifling laughter, I said, "Woody. If you are working in a barbecue stand and can't figure out how to eat lunch, I can't help you."

A few more days went by before I got another call.

"I think Grampy Mike is doing something illegal," he said.

"Really?" I asked. "What's happening?"

"Well, we are working twelve- and fourteen-hour days and it is my understanding that we're supposed to be getting time and a half for part of that."

To me this indicated that the other workers were grumbling about the hours.

"What he's doing that's illegal is that he's giving you cash at the end of the day," I told him. "If you'd like to give thirty-three percent of that to the government, then we can talk to him about time and a half."

There was a brief pause on the line as he did some mental calculations. "No," he said. "This will be alright."

The next summer, when I told him he was going to have to get a job locally or else he'd have to go back and work at the fair, he had a ready answer. "I don't want to get a job where I'll have to pay taxes!"

Just as they did with me, the lessons did eventually take hold. Now he and my daughter, Faye Landess, readily pitch in and work at events, and I get a big kick when they walk through the restaurant and make observations with an owner's lens, noticing waste, loitering employees, or anything else that seems not quite right. I knew it had all come full circle when Woody began working in the publishing industry in New York City and groused about the work habits of one of his coworkers. "She leaves at the stroke of six o'clock, no matter what we have going on!" he said. "I just don't understand how she feels okay about that!"

═Amy═

HOLY COMMUNION

BOOZY BEVERAGES WITH A BARBECUE TWIST

ANY RECIPE that starts with a case of beer and a bottle of rum (see page 269) promises a good time. Alcoholic libations—from ice-packed coolers of Bud and mason jars brimming with real moonshine to passed bottles of brown water (aka bourbon and whiskey) and red Solo cups aslosh with potent punches—shared around the burn barrel, late into the night, are a big part of the communal experience of barbecue. At competitions and festivals, an unwritten code of hospitality dictates that all who enter any team's tent are greeted with a beverage—be they old friends or arch rivals (or, as is oftentimes the case, both). On the home front, from impromptu backyard barbecue gatherings to holidays, weddings, and other put-on-the-hog special events, we have made a whole slew of cherished memories over cocktails with family and friends.

Each of the signature drinks collected in this chapter has a story behind it (some we tell; others, well . . .). In sharing these dazzling concoctions with you, we offer up a blessing: May you imbibe them in good health—and enjoy making some colorful memories of your own.

BELLY UP TO THE 17TH STREET BAR

Our bar business is pretty straightforward. We sell equal amounts of Bud Light and our own locally brewed 17ST Amber Ale, a dark beer brewed with hops smoked over cherry wood, specially designed to complement our barbecue. Curiously, despite our small size and relatively remote location, we're the number one seller of Red Hook ESB draft in the state of Illinois. There are a few local wines and a few Californians, for folks so inclined. Bourbons and whiskeys of all levels are popular and, just like barbecue, people enjoy exploring the heritage and craft behind the blends. They're also the basis for classic cocktails that are now being rediscovered and reinvented by new generations of cocktail imbibers, as well as for lots of cocktails and punches enjoyed on the competition circuit and at a variety of barbecue restaurants.

For special events, we like to be a bit more adventuresome, and we can take a bit more time. We've collected favorite cocktails over the years and have had a good time developing new combinations with our pal RH Weaver, a highly respected mixologist and bar consultant based in Charleston.

Here are some ways to make your cocktails extra special:

- Freshly juiced fruits and vegetables make for superior cocktails. You can juice citrus by hand, with a citrus reamer. For dense fruits such as pineapples, the Hurom slow juicer is our juicer of choice (see page 323). Buying top-quality juice is the second-best option.

- Grilling fruit (page 244) before juicing takes a cocktail to a whole new level.

- Simple syrup is a liquid made up of sugar and/or other sweeteners melted in water; we often infuse it with herbs or other ingredients to add surprising depth and flavor dimensions to our cocktails.

- Edge the rim of your serving glasses with colorful sugars or salts mixed with herbs or dry rubs to add extra flavor and festive color.

- Antique stores are filled with affordable and unusual cocktail glasses, barware, and accessories, all of which bring even more snazz and style to the party.

ICE ICE BABY

The quality of ice makes a huge difference in cocktails. Here's a surprisingly easy way to make a batch of crystal clear, long-lasting ice for a party. Fill a small, six-pack-size cooler three-quarters full of water and set it in the freezer overnight, with the lid open or off. The cloudy part of the water will rise to the top. When you take the ice out of the cooler the following day (after about 12 hours), it will still be a bit loose, so you can use a large chef's knife to chop off the cloudy portion, and you can pour out the water that hasn't frozen. Now you'll be left with a large block of perfectly clear glass-like ice. Put the block on a small rimmed baking sheet, use a knife to cut a groove into the ice, and tap the knife with a rubber mallet to cut through the block. Repeat to create cubes and large shards of ice. Put some in a bag and crush it or break it into smaller pieces. Make very large pieces for use in punches. Keep the ice in a bag in the freezer for future use.

HOG & HOMINY OLD-FASHIONED

MAKES 1 COCKTAIL

Every October, I travel down to Oxford, Mississippi, for the Southern Foodways Symposium. I go for the thoughtful programming that celebrates Southern food and culture, and I heartily enjoy the opportunity to feast upon amazing and inventive Southern fare. As I make my way down to Oxford, the first stop is Hog & Hominy, the Memphis restaurant owned by chefs Michael Hudman and Andy Ticer, and an unofficial clubhouse for those attending the symposium. Participants gather for sustenance and libations, and it's not uncommon to see groups of people ordering everything off the menu and passing it around, family-style. The food is outstanding, and the cocktails are an important part of the experience. The Old-Fashioned, in particular, is one of the best I've tasted. Several techniques make their version a standout. The right ice is key—they serve their cocktail with a giant ice ball that melts slowly, so the drink doesn't get watered down. Luckily, it's easy to find oversized ice molds online or in specialty food stores. Also, high-quality orange bitters make all the difference. Hog & Hominy makes their own, but a good store-bought version like Regan's will do the trick. Lastly, the order in which you add and mix the ingredients is important. —Amy

1 large strip orange zest

1 cube or ½ teaspoon Demerara sugar

3 drops high-quality orange bitters (such as Regan's)

1 drop Angostura bitters

½ ounce club soda, plus more to taste

2 ounces bourbon (we use Maker's Mark)

1 large round or square ice cube (see opposite)

Twist the zest to release its natural oils and rub it along the rim and inside of an old-fashioned glass. Place the sugar in the bottom of the glass, then add both bitters and a spritz of orange oil from the zest. Add a splash of club soda and muddle to dissolve the sugar and combine the ingredients. Pour in the bourbon and another splash of soda and stir. Add the ice and garnish with the orange zest.

A PROPER NEGRONI

MAKES 1 COCKTAIL

"The Mississippi Delta begins in the lobby of the Peabody Hotel and ends on Catfish Row in Vicksburg. The Peabody is the Paris Ritz, the Cairo Shepheard's, the London Savoy of this section. If you stand near its fountain in the middle of the lobby . . . ultimately you will see everybody who is anybody in the Delta . . ."

—Author/historian David Cohn, 1935

Relaxing over cocktails in the lobby at the Peabody Hotel in Memphis is one of life's most civilized pleasures. Some of our best memories were made during moments in this ornate, quietly elegant space while wearing dusty, smoke-infused barbecue cook-off clothes. A bit incongruous, to be sure.

Our favorite Peabody lobby partners in crime are the boys from the Ribdiculous Bar-B-Krewe team. A merry band of esteemed chefs who worked together at Craft in Manhattan, they've dispersed to all corners of the country, and competing at Memphis in May is a sacred weekend trip that none will miss. Most competitors swig beer and bourbon at their cooking sites, but Negronis are the cocktail of choice ordered at the Peabody bar. Chef and Bar-B-Krewer Shane McBride has schooled the bartenders on proper Negroni making. This is a slight twist on that beverage, with grilled orange to add a little smoky sweetness (you can obtain great flavor from charring the orange in a cast-iron pan, too).

½ orange	1 ounce gin	1 ounce Campari
Sugar	1 ounce sweet vermouth	1 large round or square ice cube (see page 252)

Preheat a grill to medium or a small cast-iron skillet over medium heat.

Dip the cut surface of the orange in sugar. Grill, sugar side down, for 3 to 4 minutes, or until the orange is caramelized and slightly charred, but not burned. Alternatively, char in a cast-iron skillet over heat for 2 to 3 minutes. If using for garnish, cut into wedges.

Combine the gin, vermouth, and Campari in an old-fashioned glass with ice. Either garnish with the grilled fruit or, using a citrus reamer, extract the juice and add. Stir and enjoy.

UBONS SPECIAL

MAKES 1 COCKTAIL

Longtime friends from the competition circuit, the Ubons barbecue family is made up of the Roarkes of Yazoo City, Mississippi, and a cast of assorted other characters. We're fortunate to meet on Madison Avenue at the Big Apple Barbecue Block Party each June. When you step into their tent, you're greeted with one of their signature fruity bourbon drinks. We've kicked their version up by using fresh juiced pineapple and pure cane sugar–sweetened citrus soda.

Ice cubes (see page 252)

2 ounces fresh pineapple juice

2 ounces Jim Beam bourbon

2 ounces cane sugar–sweetened citrus soda (we use Ski) or Sprite

Fresh pineapple spear, for garnish

Fill a tall glass with ice cubes. Combine additional ice cubes with the pineapple juice and Jim Beam in a shaker. Shake well and strain into the glass. Top with the soda. Garnish with a spear of pineapple.

PORK & STORMY

MAKES 1 COCKTAIL

Our good friend Carey Bringle, the proprietor of Peg Leg Porker out of Nashville, coined the name of this cocktail, and he makes a version with his own Peg Leg Porker Tennessee Straight Bourbon. We encourage you to use your favorite bourbon and ginger beer. We're partial to Fitz's, which we carry at 17th Street, and Blenheim ginger ale, which we carry back whenever we visit South Carolina. We've added our own touch with a cane-sugar-and-bacon bourbon floater that adds a deep, sweet, smoky flavor.

BACON-WASHED BOURBON

4 strips bacon

8 ounces bourbon (your choice)

1 teaspoon pure cane syrup (we use Lavington's, Poirier's, or Steen's; see page 19)

COCKTAIL

Ice cubes or shards (see page 252)

2 ounces bourbon (your choice)

3 ounces ginger beer

Lime wedge, for garnish

For the bacon-washed bourbon: Fry the bacon in a cast-iron skillet until crispy. Combine 2 tablespoons of the bacon grease and the bourbon in a plastic container with a lid (eat the bacon). Shake thoroughly and freeze until the fat hardens, about 1 hour. Remove from the freezer and strain the fat from the bourbon; discard the fat. Add the cane syrup to the bourbon and mix well. Decant into a covered glass jar or bottle and store in the refrigerator.

For one cocktail: Fill a cocktail glass with ice. Add the bourbon, top with the ginger beer, and stir. Add a teaspoon of the bacon-washed bourbon to the top of the drink. Garnish with a lime wedge.

17TH STREET SHUFFLE

MAKES 1 COCKTAIL

This potent, smooth cocktail mixes small-batch bourbon with notes of grapefruit and aromatic Barolo Chinato. The cocktail was created for our Whole Hog Extravaganza by Charleston-based RH Weaver, known simply as "Weaver" in the cocktail world, and it's repeated each year to much acclaim. Collaborating with Weaver on cocktails and alcohol education, with bourbon tastings and discussions on profitable bar programs for our special events and our staff, has been a gift.

Barolo Chinato is a digestif, once famed for its medicinal purposes. It's made from Barolo wine steeped with the bark from the *China calissaya* tree and flavored with up to twenty-one herbs and spices, including cinnamon, coriander, rhubarb roots, cardamom, mint, and/or vanilla, depending on the particular recipe.

1½ ounces Four Roses Bourbon Small Batch

¾ ounce Giffard Crème de Pamplemousse grapefruit liqueur

¾ ounce Barolo Chinato

Ice cubes (see page 252)

Lemon or lime zest twist, for garnish

Combine the bourbon, liqueur, and Barolo Chinato in a mixing glass. Add ice cubes and stir until chilled. Strain into a small glass filled with ice. Garnish with the zest.

SALTY PIG

MAKES 2 COCKTAILS, PLUS ABOUT 12 OUNCES SYRUP AND EXTRA ROSEMARY SALT

A traditional Salty Dog is gin or vodka with grapefruit juice and a salty rim. We give it a fresh new look by using the juice of a grilled grapefruit and creating a roasted rosemary edging salt, using both kosher and coarse sea salts for extra texture.

ROSEMARY SALT

2 tablespoons fresh rosemary leaves, stripped from the stem

2 tablespoons kosher salt

3 tablespoons coarse sea salt

Citrus wedge or grapefruit juice

DEMERARA SYRUP

1 cup Demerara sugar

COCKTAILS

2 large Ruby Red grapefruits

4 ounces vodka (your choice)

Ice cubes (see page 252)

Rosemary sprigs, for garnish

For the rosemary salt: Preheat the oven to 300°, with a rack in the center.

Pulse the rosemary in a mini food processor or blender until coarsely chopped. Add the kosher and sea salts and pulse a few more times until chopped and blended. The mixture will be slightly damp. Spread on a baking sheet and bake, watching carefully so it doesn't burn, for 8 to 10 minutes, just until dry and fragrant but not browned. Alternatively, cook, stirring, in a small skillet over medium-low heat, just until dry and fragrant, again taking care not to burn. Set aside to cool. Store in a covered glass jar.

For the syrup: Combine the sugar and 1 cup water in a small saucepan. Bring to a boil, stirring constantly for a few minutes, until the sugar is dissolved. Set aside to cool. Decant into a covered glass jar or bottle and store in the refrigerator.

For the cocktails: Spread the rosemary salt in a saucer. Rim the outer edge of two glasses with a piece of citrus or grapefruit juice and twist the rim in the rosemary salt to coat. Set aside to dry.

Cut the grapefruits in half and grill, cut side down, over medium coals for 5 to 9 minutes, until slightly charred but not burned. Alternatively, char the whole grapefruits all over in a cast-iron skillet over medium heat. Be careful not to overheat or the grapefruit may burst. Let the grapefruits cool until you can handle them. Squeeze the juice into a measuring cup (you should have about ½ cup) and set aside to cool.

Combine the grapefruit juice, 1 ounce of the Demerara syrup, and the vodka in a shaker. Add ice and shake. Double-strain into the glasses. Garnish with a sprig of rosemary.

AMY'S MARGARITA

MAKES 1 COCKTAIL

My friend John Delpha of Rosebud Kitchen in Boston whipped up a version of this for me as we were celebrating after finishing one of our OnCue classes. We refined the original with a splash of cane sugar soda and fresh grilled juices.

½ lime

½ orange

½ grapefruit

2 tablespoons kosher salt

3 tablespoons coarse sea salt

1 lime wedge

Ice shards and cubes (see page 252)

½ ounce cane sugar–sweetened citrus soda (we use Ski)

1 ounce Patrón Citrónge orange liqueur

1 ounce Cointreau orange liqueur

Lime pinwheel, for garnish

Grill the lime, orange, and grapefruit, cut side down, over medium coals for 5 to 8 minutes, or until the fruit is slightly charred but not burned. Squeeze ½ ounce juice from each fruit and set aside.

In a small bowl, combine the kosher salt and sea salt. Spread on a saucer. Rim the outer edge of a glass with a lime wedge and twist the glass rim in the salt to coat. Set aside to dry.

Fill the glass with ice shards. Combine the citrus juices, soda, Patrón, and Cointreau in a shaker. Add ice cubes and shake hard. Strain into the glass. Garnish with a lime pinwheel.

LIPSTICK ON A PIG

MAKES 1 COCKTAIL

A swizzle is a rum-based sour cocktail, mixed with a swizzle stick. Our playful riff on this Caribbean tradition is both sweet and spicy. It uses Giffard orgeat syrup, an almond syrup, and gets its bite from a pomegranate-habanero syrup (drizzle leftovers on vanilla ice cream). Red sanding sugar, often used for cookie decorating, adds an extra festive touch to the rim.

POMEGRANATE-HABANERO SYRUP

One 32-ounce bottle POM Wonderful pomegranate juice

½ cup granulated sugar

1 habanero pepper, quartered

COCKTAIL

Red sanding sugar, for edging the glass

¼ ounce fresh lime juice

1½ ounces Giffard orgeat syrup

2 ounces white rum

Ice cubes (see page 252)

Pomegranate seeds, for garnish

Lime zest twist, for garnish

For the syrup: Combine the pomegranate juice and granulated sugar in a medium saucepan over medium heat, stirring until the sugar is dissolved. Add the habanero and heat until simmering. Cook, stirring occasionally, until the liquid has reduced by half, about 30 minutes. Strain into a glass jar and set aside to cool. Discard the habanero. Decant into a mason jar and refrigerate; the syrup will keep for at least a week.

For the cocktail: Pour a little of the pomegranate-habanero syrup into a saucer. Spread the sanding sugar on another saucer. Dip the rim of a cocktail glass in the syrup, then twist the glass in the sugar crystals to coat. Set aside to dry.

Combine the lime juice, orgeat, and rum in a mixing glass. Stir to combine.

Add ice cubes to the cocktail glass, being careful to not disturb the sugar crystals. Pour the cocktail over the ice. Drizzle a teaspoon of the syrup over the top of the cocktail. Garnish with a few pomegranate seeds and a lime zest twist.

PINK PANTY PULLDOWN PUNCH

MAKES A VAT (ABOUT 58 SIX-OUNCE SERVINGS)

Nowhere is this punch more famous than in our VIP tent on Madison Avenue during the Big Apple Barbecue Block Party. Sip with caution—it's easy drinking and doesn't taste like alcohol at all. This one will catch up with you quickly!

PUNCH

One 1-liter bottle light rum (quality does not matter here)

Two 12-ounce cans pink lemonade concentrate

½ cup fresh lime juice

½ cup maraschino cherry juice

1 case (twenty-four 12-ounce cans) beer (cheap beer, like Bud Light, works best)

Maraschino cherries and lime rounds, to float in the punch

RIM COATING (OPTIONAL)

Pink sanding sugar, for edging the cups

Lime wedges

Ice cubes (see page 252)

For the punch: Mix the rum, lemonade concentrate, lime juice, and cherry juice in a large container or punchbowl until the lemonade concentrate dissolves. Add the beer and stir to combine. Float some cherries and lime rounds on top of the punch.

For coating (optional): Spread the sugar in a saucer. Rim the outer edge of each glass with lime and twist the rim in the sugar to coat. Set aside to dry.

Add ice cubes to each glass. Ladle the punch over the ice, being careful not to disturb the sugar rims. Garnish with cherries.

BLOOD ORANGE MARGARITA PUNCH

MAKES ABOUT 24 SIX-OUNCE SERVINGS

Any good juice orange will combine well with blood oranges in this punch, but if Cara Cara oranges are in season, use those for extra bright sweetness. Grilling the citrus intensifies its flavor, and infusing the agave syrup and simple syrup with jalapeño and cilantro, respectively, adds a subtle depth that makes this cocktail extra special.

Agave syrup is available in most grocery stores, near the sugar and other sweeteners.

8 blood oranges

12 juice oranges

48 ounces (1½ liters) plata tequila (we use Hornitos)

16 ounces fresh lime juice

24 ounces Jalapeño-Infused Agave Syrup (recipe follows)

8 ounces Cilantro Simple Syrup (recipe follows)

Ice cubes (see page 252)

Serrano pepper slivers, for garnish

Fresh cilantro leaves, for garnish

Cut the oranges in half and grill, cut side down, over medium coals, in batches if necessary, for 5 to 8 minutes, or until the oranges are slightly browned, but not burned. Alternatively, char whole oranges in batches in a cast-iron skillet over medium heat. Char the peel, but be careful not to overheat or the oranges may burst.

Juice the oranges into a large container or punchbowl. Add the tequila, lime juice, jalapeño syrup, and cilantro syrup and stir well. Chill until you're ready to serve.

For each serving, add ice to a glass, ladle in the punch, and garnish with slivers of serrano pepper and cilantro leaves.

(continued)

↓

Jalapeño-Infused Agave Syrup

MAKES ABOUT 24 OUNCES

3 cups agave syrup
1 large jalapeño pepper, quartered

Bring the agave syrup, 1¼ cups water, and the jalapeño to a boil in a medium saucepan. Reduce the heat to a simmer and cook for about 30 minutes, or until the mixture is reduced to 3 cups. Take the pan off the heat, strain, and let cool. Decant into a jar, cover, and store in the refrigerator.

Cilantro Simple Syrup

MAKES ABOUT 12 OUNCES

1 cup sugar
½ cup chopped fresh cilantro

Bring 1 cup water and the sugar to a boil in a medium saucepan. Turn off the heat and add the cilantro, stirring 2 or 3 times. Take the pan off the heat and let cool. Strain into a covered glass jar or bottle and store in the refrigerator.

CHARLESTON BROWN WATER SOCIETY PUNCH

MAKES A VAT (ABOUT 30 SIX-OUNCE SERVINGS)

Charleston has become somewhat of a third home to us, and we've spent a good deal of time with the fun-loving members of the Charleston Brown Water Society. This convivial crew is a society chartered to share spirits knowledge and raise money for educational scholarships. They created this delicious punch to celebrate Charleston's rich spirit of hospitality.

Honey Simple Syrup (recipe follows)

Demerara Simple Syrup (recipe follows)

Two 1-liter bottles Old Forester Signature 100-Proof bourbon

One 1-liter bottle Mount Gay Barbados rum

32 ounces fresh orange juice

4 ounces fresh lemon juice

8 ounces cold club soda, plus more as needed

Orange slices, for garnish

One day in advance, make an ice mold using a Bundt pan or other baking dish suitable in size to that of the container in which you'll be serving the punch. (A large piece of ice melts more slowly and won't water down the punch.)

Pour the honey syrup, Demerara syrup, bourbon, rum, and orange and lemon juices into a large container or punchbowl. Stir to combine. Carefully add the ice block. Add club soda to taste and garnish with orange slices. Ladle into individual glasses and serve.

(continued)

↓

Charleston Brown Water Society Punch

Honey Simple Syrup

MAKES 16 OUNCES

1 cup honey, preferably local

Combine the honey and 1 cup water in a small saucepan and bring to a boil, stirring constantly for several minutes. Take the pan off the heat and set aside to cool. Decant into a mason jar and refrigerate; the syrup will keep for at least a week.

Demerara Simple Syrup

MAKES 16 OUNCES

1 cup Demerara sugar

Combine the sugar and 1 cup water in a small saucepan and bring to a boil, stirring constantly, for several minutes, until the sugar dissolves. Take the pan off the heat and set aside to cool. Decant into a mason jar and refrigerate; the syrup will keep for at least a week.

MAGIC MARY BAR

MAKES ENOUGH BASE FOR 12 TO 16 BLOODY MARYS

The Magic Mary, edged with Pure Magic and with a little barbecue sauce added to the mix, is our version of a Bloody Mary. A Magic Mary bar is one of our favorite ways to entertain, and adds a festive note to any party or celebration. There's no limit to the number of interesting and delicious items you can use to garnish the cocktails (see below). Make up your own creative skewers or let guests have fun designing their own. Most bartenders swear by Zing Zang Bloody Mary mix, and that's what we use at 17th Street, adding a few items to amp up the flavor and make it our own. Two kinds of salt make for extra texture on the rim of the glass.

RIM COATING

2 tablespoons kosher salt

2 tablespoons coarse sea salt

1 teaspoon Pure Magic dry rub (page 29) or your choice

Lime or lemon wedges

BASE

Two 32-ounce bottles Zing Zang Bloody Mary Mix

One 32-ounce bottle Clamato juice

PER SERVING

1½ ounces vodka (we use Tito's)

¼ teaspoon celery salt

¼ teaspoon freshly ground black pepper

¼ teaspoon Pure Magic dry rub (page 29) or your choice

2 teaspoons barbecue sauce (your choice)

1 teaspoon prepared horseradish

1 teaspoon Worcestershire sauce

1 teaspoon dill pickle juice

1 teaspoon 17th Street Wing Sauce (page 56; optional, to make it spicier)

GARNISHES

Slices of sausage

Cheese cubes

Pickled okra

Dilled green beans

Dill pickles

Sweet pickles

Pickled asparagus

Pickled onions

Pepperoncini peppers

Celery sticks

Cherry tomatoes

Beef jerky sticks

Lacquered Bacon (page 50)

Lemon wedges

Lime wedges

4- to 6-inch wooden skewers

For the coating: Combine the kosher salt, sea salt, and dry rub in a small bowl, then spread it on a saucer.

For the base: Mix the Bloody Mary mix and Clamato juice in a large pitcher. Chill in the refrigerator.

(continued)

↓

For one Bloody Mary: Rub the outer rim of a tall glass with a lime wedge and twist the glass on the saucer to coat with the dry rub–salt mixture. Set aside to dry.

Add ice and the vodka to a shaker. Sprinkle the celery salt, pepper, and dry rub over the top of the ice. Add the barbecue sauce, horseradish, Worcestershire sauce, dill pickle juice, and wing sauce, if desired. Add 6 to 8 ounces of the base. Shake vigorously and pour into the prepared glass. Garnish as desired. Guests can thread cheese, sausage, and pickled garnishes of their choice onto the wooden skewers and add celery sticks, tomatoes, jerky, bacon, and citrus wedges as desired.

BENEDICTION

DIVINE DESSERTS AND SWEET SALVATION

OUR FAMILY is big on dessert, and many of the recipes in this chapter are treasured heirlooms. In baking, as in barbecuing, we have very particular opinions about the correct way of doing things. From the time that I was very young, I was schooled by my grandmother Mama Faye and my Aunt Jeanette in making dessert. Among their edicts: Piecrust makes or breaks any dessert of which it is a part (and in our neck of the woods, this includes strawberry shortcake); nothing beats a well-made, pure and simple white cake; and the peaches and apples grown in Southern Illinois are unquestionably superior to those in any other part of the country.

We do indeed live smack in the middle of the finest fruit farms and orchards, where strawberry, blackberry, peach, and apple seasons tumble into one another, and much of our day-to-day baking offers up this blessed bounty in pies and tarts. Along with those stalwarts, we share with you a few decidedly unique regional favorites, such as the confusingly named peanut rolls and the distinctly St. Louis classic, Gooey Butter Cake. We hope they become favorites in your family, too. ⥱Amy⥲

STRAWBERRY SHORTCAKE, SOUTHERN ILLINOIS–STYLE

MAKES 8 TO 10 SERVINGS

Our way of making certain dishes is part of the fabric of our family and creates our own family traditions and food memories. Growing up, we used piecrust for strawberry shortcake, and not until I was older did I realize that other people used biscuits, sponge cake, or angel food cake. Tippey's, a diner that was open for forty years in Murphysboro, made their strawberry shortcake this way, and the Lodge at Giant City State Park serves strawberry shortcake this way as well. We take a big group of friends to the Lodge on the Sunday following our barbecue cook-off each September, and they always marvel at this rendition. —Amy

PIECRUST

2½ cups all-purpose flour (we use King Arthur), plus more for rolling

1½ teaspoons granulated sugar

1 teaspoon kosher salt

8 tablespoons (1 stick) cold unsalted butter, cut into cubes

½ cup cold lard

About 5 tablespoons ice water

1 tablespoon coarse sugar, for sprinkling

2 quarts strawberries, hulled, washed, and dried thoroughly

¼ cup sugar, plus more to taste

Whipped cream, for serving

For the piecrust: Put the flour, granulated sugar, and salt in a food processor and pulse to mix. Add the butter and lard and pulse gently until it resembles coarse crumbs. Be careful not to overmix. Sprinkle in the ice water, a tablespoon at a time, and pulse just until the mixture gathers into a dough.

Divide the dough in half, shape into 2 balls, flatten into disks, and wrap each in plastic wrap. Refrigerate for at least 1 hour.

Preheat the oven to 350°, with a rack in the center. Line 2 baking sheets with parchment paper.

Lightly flour the work surface. Roll out one dough disk to an ⅛-inch-thick rectangle. Sprinkle with coarse sugar and cut into 6-x-2-inch strips. Using a spatula, transfer the strips to the baking sheets. Repeat with the second disk. Bake 15 to 20 minutes, until golden brown. Cool on a wire rack.

(continued)
↓

Coarsely chop the strawberries and transfer half of them to a medium bowl. Place the remaining strawberries in a food processor and sprinkle with the sugar. Pulse gently until finely chopped. Alternatively, use a serrated biscuit cutter to finely chop the berries. Add these to the coarsely chopped berries and mix to combine. Sprinkle with a little more sugar if necessary. Cover and macerate in the refrigerator for about 1 hour.

For each serving, break 1 piecrust strip into pieces and place in a bowl. Spoon strawberries on top, add a few more pieces of piecrust, and top with whipped cream.

PEACH HAND PIES

MAKES 12

Southern Illinois is home to half a dozen orchards where some of the finest peaches and apples in the world are grown. Peach season is relatively short, and we take full advantage, making shortcake, pies, and cobblers, or just eating them over the sink, with the juices running down our fingers. Hand pies are a favorite. If you can't get good, fresh peaches, don't waste your time. Instead, substitute another fruit or berry that's ripe and in season.

PIECRUST

2½ cups all-purpose flour (we use King Arthur), plus more for rolling

1½ teaspoons granulated sugar

1 teaspoon kosher salt

8 tablespoons (1 stick) cold unsalted butter, cut into cubes

½ cup cold lard

5 tablespoons ice water

4 cups sliced peaches (6 to 8 soft, ripe peaches, pitted)

2 tablespoons granulated sugar

1 tablespoon light brown sugar

1 teaspoon ground cinnamon

1 tablespoon grated lemon zest

1 tablespoon fresh lemon juice

1 large egg

Sparkling sugar or granulated sugar, for sprinkling

For the piecrust: Put the flour, granulated sugar, and salt in a food processor and pulse to mix. Add the butter and lard and pulse gently until it resembles coarse crumbs. Be careful not to overmix. Sprinkle in the water, a tablespoon at a time, and pulse just until the mixture gathers into a dough.

Divide the dough in half, shape into 2 balls, flatten into disks, and wrap each in plastic wrap. Refrigerate for at least 1 hour.

Preheat the oven to 400°, with a rack in the center. Line a baking sheet with parchment paper.

Cut the peach slices into ½-inch squares. In a large bowl, combine the peaches, granulated sugar, brown sugar, cinnamon, lemon zest, and lemon juice.

Whisk the egg and 1 tablespoon water in a small bowl to make an egg wash.

(continued)
↓

Lightly flour the work surface. Roll out one pastry disk into a 14-inch round, about ⅛ inch thick. Use a saucer as a pattern and cut six 6-inch circles. Divide half of the peach filling among the circles, mounding the filling on one half of each circle. Brush the egg wash on the edge of the circles. Fold the piecrust over the filling, pressing gently to seal and using a fork to gently crimp the edges. Repeat with the remaining piecrust and filling.

Brush the top of each pie with the egg wash. Sprinkle with sparkling sugar. Cut a slit in the top of each pie to allow steam to release. Arrange the pies on the baking sheets. Bake 18 to 20 minutes, until golden brown. Transfer to a wire rack to cool.

Cool for at least 10 minutes before serving.

BLACKBERRY SLAB PIE

MAKES 12 SERVINGS

Blackberry season is a favorite time of year and luckily, it coincides with my birthday in July. My sister, Jeanette, always made a blackberry pie or cobbler. We're particular about pies in our family, and hers were the best. She never measured when she baked, and she made the flakiest piecrust just by feel. Her husband, John, never liked seeing her pies go out of the house, but he always made a grudging exception if it was coming to me, and for that I am grateful. — Mike

PIECRUST

5 cups all-purpose flour (we use King Arthur), plus more for rolling

1 tablespoon granulated sugar

2 teaspoons kosher salt

½ pound (2 sticks) cold unsalted butter, cut into cubes

1 cup cold lard

½ cup plus 2 tablespoons ice water

8 pints blackberries

⅔ cup granulated sugar

¾ cup all-purpose flour

2 teaspoons grated lemon zest

¼ cup fresh lemon juice

1 large egg

8 tablespoons (1 stick) cold unsalted butter, cut into cubes

Sparkling sugar or granulated sugar, for sprinkling

For the piecrust: Put the flour, granulated sugar, and salt in a food processor and pulse to mix. Add the butter and lard and pulse gently until it resembles coarse crumbs. Be careful not to overmix. Sprinkle in the ice water, a tablespoon at a time, and pulse just until the mixture gathers into a dough.

Divide the pastry in half and shape into 2 balls, one a bit larger than the other. Flatten the balls into disks, wrap each in plastic wrap, and refrigerate for at least 1 hour.

Stir together the blackberries, granulated sugar, flour, lemon zest, and lemon juice in a large bowl.

Whisk the egg and 1 tablespoon water in a small bowl to make an egg wash.

Preheat the oven to 425°, with a rack in the center. If you have a baking sheet larger than 13 x 9 inches, place it on the bottom rack; if not, line the bottom rack with aluminum foil. (This will catch any drips as the pie bakes.)

(continued)

↓

Lightly flour the work surface. Roll out the larger pastry disk to an 18-x-13-inch rectangle. The piecrust should be about ⅛ inch thick. Transfer to a 13-x-9-inch baking dish. Gently press the crust into the pan and up the sides; you may have to pleat it a little at the corners.

Roll the remaining pastry out to a circle that is 11 inches in diameter and cut it into ½-inch-wide strips.

Scrape the blackberry filling into the bottom crust and dot the surface with the butter cubes. Arrange the strips of dough in a pattern on top of the filling. Trim off the excess and crimp the edges. Brush the top and edges with the egg wash and sprinkle with sparkling sugar.

Bake for 15 minutes, then lower the temperature to 375° and continue baking for 45 minutes, or until the crust is golden and the fruit is bubbling. If the edges begin to get too brown, cover with strips of foil. Let the pie cool and set for at least 4 hours before serving.

RUSTIC APPLE CRANBERRY TART

MAKES ONE 10-INCH TART

Apples and cranberries are my favorite combination of fall fruit, and the bright, tart cranberries keep this dessert from being too sweet. Adapted from a recipe taught to me by my friend Joanna McGee, this has long been my Thanksgiving and Christmas dessert staple, and it's as festive as it is delicious. I always hope there's a bit left over so I can enjoy it the next morning with my coffee. —Amy

CREAM CHEESE PASTRY

One 8-ounce package cream cheese, at room temperature

½ pound (2 sticks) unsalted butter, cut into pieces, softened

2 cups all-purpose flour (we use King Arthur), plus 1 to 2 tablespoons more as needed

½ teaspoon kosher salt

FILLING

1 orange

2 tablespoons cornstarch

3 cups (one 12-ounce bag) whole fresh cranberries, rinsed, picked over, and blotted dry

2 large Granny Smith apples (or your choice of baking apple), peeled, cored, and chopped into ½-inch bits

½ cup golden raisins

1 cup packed light brown sugar

½ teaspoon ground cinnamon

½ teaspoon freshly grated nutmeg

½ cup chopped walnuts

½ cup orange marmalade

EGG GLAZE

1 large egg, beaten with 1 teaspoon water

1 tablespoon coarse or sparkling sugar

JAM GLAZE

½ cup seedless red currant jam

For the pastry: Combine the cream cheese and butter in a food processor and process until creamy; add the flour and salt and pulse just until the dough begins to clump. Lightly flour the work surface. Turn out the dough onto the work surface and form into a ball. It should feel soft, but not sticky. If it feels sticky, gently work in a tablespoon or two more flour. Form the pastry into a flat disk about 1 inch thick. Wrap in plastic and refrigerate for at least 30 minutes.

Preheat the oven to 425°, with a rack in the lower third.

For the filling: Finely grate the orange zest; you'll need 2 teaspoons. Set the zest aside. Squeeze ⅓ cup juice into a small bowl. Add the cornstarch and whisk together until the cornstarch dissolves.

(continued)

↓

In a large bowl, toss together the cranberries, apples, raisins, orange zest, brown sugar, cinnamon, nutmeg, and walnuts. Add the marmalade and the cornstarch mixture and stir to combine.

Place a sheet of aluminum foil on a baking sheet and grease the foil. Soften the pastry at room temperature for about 5 minutes; if it is too cold, it may crack or break. Unwrap and place it in the center of a piece of parchment paper. Lightly flour the rolling pin and roll the pastry into a 16-inch circle.

Slide the pastry, still on the parchment paper, onto a baking sheet. Use a pastry brush to lightly brush the egg glaze all over the pastry. Scrape the fruit into the center, leaving a 2-inch border. Roll in the edge of the pastry about 3 inches all around to cover the edges of the fruit and create a rim. Brush any cracks with some of the egg glaze and pinch them together. Brush the folded-over crust with egg glaze and sprinkle with sugar.

Turn up the edges of the foil to create a rim that will help catch any juices that escape while the tart is baking.

Bake the tart for 15 minutes. Lower the temperature to 350° and bake for another 25 to 30 minutes, until the pastry is golden brown. If the edges begin to get too brown too early, or the fruit begins to look too dark, cover with foil.

Slide the foil holding the tart off the baking sheet and onto a wire rack to cool.

In a small saucepan, melt the jam over low heat. Using a pastry brush, brush the jam over the fruit.

Allow to cool for 30 minutes. Carefully slide the tart onto a cake stand or serving plate. Use a large spatula to lift it so you can remove the parchment paper or simply tear away all the visible edges.

FLOSSIE'S COCONUT CREAM PIE

MAKES ONE 9-INCH PIE

I order coconut cream pie anytime I see it on a menu, and I always measure it against two family favorites—one made by my maternal great-grandmother Flossie Varnum, and one made by Virginia Heern at Tippey's Restaurant, a longtime Murphysboro staple that sadly closed its doors in 2014. My favorite thing about Grandma Varnum's pie was that she chopped the coconut into smaller pieces, and there were no stringy bits throughout the custard. Some coconut cream pies have a whipped cream topping, but our family prefers a light and fluffy meringue. —Amy

SINGLE PIECRUST

1¼ cups all-purpose flour (we use King Arthur)

1 teaspoon sugar

½ teaspoon kosher salt

4 tablespoons (½ stick) cold unsalted butter, cut into cubes

¼ cup cold lard

3 to 4 tablespoons ice water

COCONUT CUSTARD

1½ cups unsweetened coconut milk

1½ cups half-and-half

5 large egg yolks (3 whites reserved for the meringue)

¾ cup sugar

¼ cup cornstarch

1 tablespoon unsalted butter

¼ teaspoon kosher salt

½ teaspoon vanilla extract

1½ cups shredded coconut (preferably unsweetened; if using sweetened, pulse in a food processor to chop into smaller pieces)

MERINGUE TOPPING

3 large egg whites

¼ teaspoon cream of tartar

6 tablespoons sugar

½ cup sweetened flaked coconut

For the piecrust: Combine the flour, sugar, and salt in a food processor and pulse to mix. Add the butter and lard and pulse gently until it resembles coarse crumbs. Be careful not to overmix. Sprinkle in the water, a tablespoon at a time, and pulse just until the mixture gathers into a dough. Shape the dough into a flat disk, wrap in plastic wrap, and refrigerate for at least 1 hour.

Lightly flour the work surface. Roll out the pastry to a 12-inch circle, about ⅛ inch thick, and fit into a 9-inch pie plate. Crimp the edges and prick the bottom of the crust all over with a fork. Freeze until firm, about 20 minutes.

While the crust freezes, preheat the oven to 375°, with a rack in the center.

(continued)

↓

Line the pastry with parchment paper cut to fit and fill with pie weights or dried beans. Bake for 20 minutes, or until the edges are golden brown. Remove the parchment paper and pie weights and bake for another 5 to 7 minutes, until the bottom is golden and dry. Transfer to a wire rack to cool.

For the custard: Pour the coconut milk and half-and-half into a 4-cup liquid measuring cup or a medium bowl. Add the egg yolks and whisk to combine. Combine the sugar and cornstarch in a large saucepan and place over medium heat. Whisk the liquid together once more and slowly pour into the saucepan, continually whisking to incorporate the sugar and cornstarch. Bring to a boil and cook, stirring and scraping the sides with a rubber spatula. Boil for 1 minute. Take the pan off the heat and stir in the butter, salt, vanilla, and coconut.

Pour the custard into the piecrust. Cover with a piece of plastic wrap, pressing down into the custard to prevent a skin from forming. Refrigerate for at least 4 hours.

Preheat the oven to 350°, with a rack in the center.

For the meringue: Beat the egg whites and cream of tartar in a medium bowl with a hand mixer on medium speed until foamy. Gradually add the sugar, 1 tablespoon at a time, beating on high after each addition, until the sugar is dissolved. Continue beating until soft, glossy peaks form.

Spread the meringue evenly over the custard, right up to the crust. Use the spatula to form peaks all over the top. Sprinkle with the coconut. Bake for 12 to 15 minutes, until the meringue is golden. Cool on a wire rack for at least 30 minutes prior to serving.

MINI MASON JAR CHEESECAKES

MAKES 6

Festive enough for a party, these are easy to assemble and a perfect sweet bite to end a meal. We used blueberries in this recipe, but they are equally good with strawberries, blackberries, or raspberries; adjust the amount of sugar to suit the sweetness of the fruit.

BERRY TOPPING

1 cup blueberries

1 cup granulated sugar

Juice of 1 lemon

1 teaspoon cornstarch

CRUST

1 cup graham cracker crumbs (9 whole graham crackers)

1 cup powdered sugar

½ teaspoon finely grated lemon zest

6 tablespoons (¾ stick) unsalted butter, melted

FILLING

One 8-ounce package cream cheese, at room temperature

1 cup heavy whipping cream

1 teaspoon vanilla extract

1 teaspoon finely grated lemon zest

Whipped cream, for garnish

1½ teaspoons finely grated lemon zest, for garnish

Twelve 4-ounce mason jars or six 8-ounce mason jars

Preheat the oven to 350°, with a rack in the center.

For the berry topping: Combine the blueberries, sugar, and lemon juice in a small saucepan over medium-low heat and cook, stirring often, for a few minutes, until the berries release their juice and the sugar dissolves. Mix the cornstarch and 2 teaspoons water in a small bowl; add to the berries and continue cooking for a few more minutes, stirring often, until the mixture thickens slightly to a syrupy consistency. Take the pan off the heat and set aside to cool to room temperature.

For the crust: In a small bowl, whisk together the graham cracker crumbs, powdered sugar, and ½ teaspoon lemon zest. Add the butter and stir to create a crumbly mixture. Divide the crust evenly among the mason jars and press lightly with your fingers or the back of a spoon to form a smooth layer. Set the jars in a small baking dish (8-inch square works well) and bake 8 to 10 minutes, just until set. Transfer to a wire rack and let cool to room temperature.

For the filling: Use a handheld electric mixer on medium-low speed to beat the cream cheese in a medium bowl until soft and creamy. Slowly add the whipping cream and continue beating on medium-low just until the mixture forms firm peaks, being careful not to overmix—it should be very smooth and creamy. Fold in the vanilla and 1 teaspoon lemon zest. Evenly divide the filling among the jars, using a butter knife or small spatula to lightly press it down to meet the crust. The filling should come up to about ½ inch to 1 inch below the top edge of the jar. Chill until you're ready to serve.

Just before serving, spoon the berry topping over the filling of each cheesecake. Top with whipped cream and sprinkle with lemon zest.

SNOOT CUPCAKES

MAKES 12

These cupcakes with their piggy noses are an easy entertaining dessert, and they make an adorable addition to a barbecue buffet.

1½ cups all-purpose flour (we use White Lily)

1½ teaspoons baking powder

¼ teaspoon kosher salt

8 tablespoons (1 stick) unsalted butter, softened

1 cup sugar

2 large eggs, separated, at room temperature

½ cup whole milk, at room temperature

½ teaspoon vanilla extract

Pink gel food coloring

Buttercream Icing (page 307)

24 chocolate chips, for topping

Preheat the oven to 350°, with a rack in the center. Line a 12-cup cupcake tin with paper liners.

In a medium bowl, sift together the flour, baking powder, and salt. In a large bowl, with an electric mixer on medium speed, beat the butter and sugar for 2 to 3 minutes, until light and fluffy. Add the egg yolks one at a time, with the mixer on low speed, scraping the bowl between additions. Beat on high speed for 2 minutes more; the mixture should be fluffy.

Alternate adding the flour mixture and the milk, starting and ending with the flour. Mix on low speed after each addition, just until incorporated. Stir in the vanilla.

In a separate bowl, with clean beaters, beat the egg whites until stiff peaks form. Gently fold one-third of the egg whites at a time into the batter. Fill each cupcake liner about one-third full. Bake for 14 to 16 minutes, until a toothpick inserted in the center of a cupcake comes out clean. Transfer the cupcake tin to a wire rack to cool completely.

Mix drops of food coloring into the buttercream until the desired shade of pink is achieved. Spoon the buttercream into a pastry bag with a plain tip or a plastic bag with a corner snipped off. Pipe icing onto each cupcake. Using a small offset spatula or butter knife, smooth the icing around the edges and across the top. Place 2 chocolate chips in the center of each cupcake.

CHURCH COOKBOOK PEANUT ROLLS

MAKES 24 CAKES, EACH ABOUT 2 INCHES SQUARE

Peanut rolls—blocks of dense sponge cake, glazed with a thin sugary icing and rolled in chopped salty peanuts—are a traditional treat in Southern Illinois and parts of Missouri. We've never seen them anywhere else.

Selling peanut rolls by the dozen is a popular fund-raiser for churches and 4-H groups in Murphysboro. Often the ladies auxiliary will get together for assembly line production: slicing whole cakes, icing the pieces, rolling them in nuts, and packaging the finished rolls for distribution. Each group has its own version—the difference might be in the texture of the cake, the size or shape of the slices, or the type and texture of the peanuts.

We've adapted this particular recipe from Murphysboro's very own LaDonna Stanton and dearly departed Lucille Reeder. The peanuts are important; quality and freshness make a big difference in the texture and taste. Mrs. Reeder always used finely ground skin-on Spanish peanuts. We favor Virginia Diner peanuts (see Resources, page 321), finely chopped and lightly toasted, for an extra salty, crunchy peanut coating. Any brand of fresh salted peanuts will do.

CAKE

2 cups all-purpose flour (we use White Lily)

2 teaspoons baking powder

¼ teaspoon kosher salt

4 large eggs, at room temperature

2 cups granulated sugar

1 cup boiling water

1 teaspoon vanilla extract, overflowing

PEANUTS AND ICING

4 cups salted peanuts

4 cups powdered sugar

2 tablespoons unsalted butter, softened

½ teaspoon vanilla extract

5 tablespoons half-and-half, plus more if needed

For the cake: Cut lengths of parchment paper or waxed paper long enough to line the bottom and sides, with overhang, of a 9-x-12-x-2-inch baking pan. Crease the parchment paper at the corners of the pan so it fits snugly.

Preheat the oven to 350°, with a rack in the center.

Sift together the flour, baking powder, and salt into a medium bowl. Beat the eggs in a large bowl with an electric mixer on medium speed until very foamy, about

3 minutes. Gradually beat in the granulated sugar until pale, thick, and satiny. Slowly add the boiling water and vanilla and mix to incorporate. Fold in the flour mixture and gently mix until thoroughly combined. Scrape the batter into the pan and smooth the top with a spatula.

Bake for 35 to 40 minutes, until the edges begin to pull away from the pan. Transfer to a wire rack to cool the cake in the pan. (Do not turn the oven off.) When completely cool, freeze for at least 2 hours before cutting.

To toast and finely chop the peanuts: Spread the peanuts in a single layer on a baking sheet. Bake for 8 to 10 minutes, until golden brown. Transfer the baking sheet to a wire rack to cool for at least 10 minutes. Chop the peanuts by pulsing 5 or 6 times in a food processor, being careful not to overprocess. Alternatively, put them in a heavy-duty plastic bag and seal it. Lay it on a cutting board and smooth the nuts to a single flat layer. Using a rolling pin or a heavy skillet, whack the nuts several times to crush them. Spread the peanuts on a plate or baking sheet.

For the icing: Sift the powdered sugar into a large bowl. Whisk in the butter and vanilla. Add the half-and-half a few teaspoons at a time, until the desired consistency is reached. The icing should be just a little heavier than a glaze used for drizzling; it needs to completely coat the cake and be heavy enough for the peanuts to adhere.

Use the parchment paper to lift the cake from the pan. Place it on a cutting board and cut into 24 rectangular pieces.

Working with one piece of cake at a time, completely ice the top and sides. Invert the cake onto the peanuts, pressing down to help the peanuts stick. Turn each side in the peanuts to coat. Ice the bottom of each cake and place in the peanuts again, or simply sprinkle thoroughly with peanuts. The entire piece of cake should be coated.

Either wrap the rolls separately in waxed paper or layer them in an airtight container with waxed paper between the sides of the rolls and between each layer. Store in the refrigerator. The cakes may be separated by waxed paper, placed in freezer bags, and frozen for up to 1 month.

FAYE LANDESS'S FANCY CAKE

MAKES ABOUT 12 SERVINGS

There's much to be said for the pure, fresh flavor of a pristine white cake. My daughter, Faye Landess, always requests this almond-scented cake for her January birthday, and I usually add something a little special, such as a layer of berries or lemon curd. A few years ago I began experimenting with ombré cakes, and I loved the look of surprise on her face when the simple cake was cut, revealing shades of her favorite color inside. This recipe includes almond extract, but you can leave that out if you prefer a more vanilla-scented cake. —Amy

1½ cups all-purpose flour (we use White Lily), plus more for the pans

1½ teaspoons baking powder

¼ teaspoon kosher salt

8 tablespoons (1 stick) unsalted butter, softened

1 cup sugar

2 large eggs, separated, at room temperature

½ cup whole milk, at room temperature

½ teaspoon vanilla extract

½ teaspoon almond extract

Purple gel food coloring

Buttercream Icing (recipe follows)

Preheat the oven to 350°, with a rack in the center and one in the top third. Grease and flour three 8-inch cake pans.

Sift together the flour, baking powder, and salt into a medium bowl. In a large bowl, with an electric mixer on medium speed, beat the butter and sugar for 2 to 3 minutes, until light and fluffy. Add the egg yolks one at a time, with the mixer on low speed, scraping the bowl between additions. Beat at high speed for 2 minutes more; the batter will become fluffy. Mixing on low speed, alternate adding the flour and milk in three additions, starting and ending with the flour, and mixing just until incorporated after each addition. Stir in the vanilla and the almond extract.

In a separate bowl, with clean beaters, beat the egg whites until stiff peaks form. Gently fold one-third of the egg whites at a time into the batter.

Divide the batter equally between three bowls. Using the food coloring, tint each bowl a different shade of purple. Mix well to incorporate all the food coloring, but take care not to deflate the batter. Pour one color into each of the cake pans.

(continued)

↓

Bake in the center and top third of the oven for 28 to 30 minutes, rotating the cakes from front to back and top to bottom at the halfway mark, until a toothpick inserted in the center comes out clean.

Cool the cakes in the pans for 5 minutes, then invert onto a wire rack and cool completely, at least 1 hour.

Using a large serrated knife, cut the dome off the tops of the darker two layers. Place the darkest layer, cut side down, on a cake stand or serving plate. Spread a coating of icing on the top. Place the second-darkest layer on top, cut side down; spread with a coat of icing, followed by the lightest purple cake layer, bottom side down.

Spread a thin coating of icing over the entire cake and let it set. Spread a final, thicker coating of icing over the entire cake. Using a small offset spatula or butter knife, smooth the icing around the edges and across the top.

Buttercream Icing

MAKES 2 CUPS

½ pound (2 sticks) unsalted butter, softened

¼ teaspoon kosher salt

2 pounds powdered sugar

6 to 7 tablespoons whole milk

1 tablespoon vanilla extract

Beat the butter and salt in a large bowl with an electric mixer on medium speed for 1 to 2 minutes, until creamy. Gradually add the sugar, alternating with 6 tablespoons of the milk, mixing on low speed after each addition, until well combined and smooth. Stir in the vanilla. Mix in the remaining 1 tablespoon milk, a bit at a time, until the frosting is smooth and creamy.

BUFFALO TRACE BROWNIE CAKE

MAKES 8 SERVINGS

This flourless chocolate cake laced with one of our favorite whiskeys is baked for a short time so it has a gooey consistency with a distinctly boozy whiff.

18 ounces best-quality semisweet chocolate (we use Guittard), coarsely chopped

½ pound (2 sticks) unsalted butter, softened

6 large eggs, at room temperature

2 tablespoons Buffalo Trace Kentucky Straight bourbon whiskey, or your choice

1 teaspoon vanilla extract

Flaky sea salt (such as Maldon's) or powdered sugar, for sprinkling

Preheat the oven to 425°, with a rack in the center. Spray a 9-inch springform pan with nonstick cooking spray and wrap the outside with aluminum foil. Fill a 13-x-9-inch baking dish with water and put it on the lower rack in the oven.

Melt the chocolate and butter in the top of a double boiler or a small saucepan set over gently simmering water in a larger one. Mix well and set aside to cool slightly.

Beat the eggs in a large bowl with an electric mixer on medium-high speed for 5 minutes, until thick and creamy. Fold in half of the melted chocolate mixture, then add the bourbon and vanilla and fold in the remaining chocolate. Pour the batter into the springform pan. Set it on the center rack above the water.

Bake 12 to 14 minutes, just until set; do not overbake. Turn off the oven and let the cake sit in the oven, with the door propped open, for 5 minutes.

Serve at room temperature. Finish with sea salt or powdered sugar.

GOOEY BUTTER CAKE

MAKES 18 PIECES

Biting into this rich, decadent cake takes me right back to my Nana's kitchen. Nana, my maternal grandmother, lived just outside St. Louis, and when I spent time at her house, she often served me a square of this regional St. Louis specialty along with a cup of coffee that was mostly half-and-half and sugar. No wonder I developed such a sweet tooth. —Amy

CRUST

3 cups all-purpose flour (we use White Lily)

1 tablespoon baking powder

½ cup powdered whole milk

2 cups granulated sugar

2 large eggs

8 tablespoons (1 stick) unsalted butter, melted and cooled

FILLING

One 8-ounce package cream cheese, softened

8 tablespoons (1 stick) unsalted butter, melted and cooled

1 teaspoon vanilla

2 large eggs

2 cups powdered sugar, sifted, plus more for sprinkling

Preheat the oven to 350°, with a rack positioned in the center. Grease one 9-x-13-inch baking pan or two 8-inch square baking pans.

For the crust: Sift the flour and baking powder together into a large mixing bowl or the bowl of a stand mixer. Whisk the powdered milk and granulated sugar into the flour mixture.

In a separate small bowl, whisk the eggs into the melted butter until smooth and creamy.

Using a stand mixer or handheld electric mixer, slowly add the wet ingredients to the dry, pausing to scrape down the bowl a couple times. Continue mixing just until a dough forms and gathers into a single mass.

Press the dough evenly over the bottom of the prepared baking pan and about 1 to 1½ inches up the sides. (If using two 8-inch square pans, divide the dough evenly between them.) Chill in the refrigerator while you make the filling.

For the filling: Using the stand mixer or handheld electric mixer, beat the cream cheese on low speed, just until smooth and creamy. Add the butter and mix on

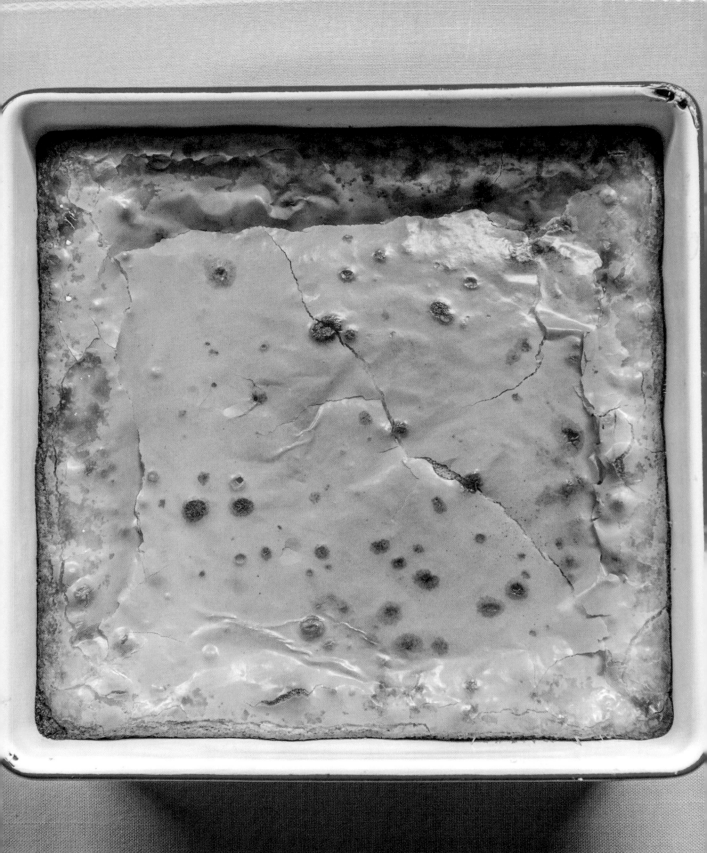

low to incorporate. Add the vanilla, then add the eggs, one at a time, continuing to mix on low speed. Gradually add the powdered sugar, mixing until thoroughly combined.

Scrape the filling into the baking pan or pans and spread evenly over the dough.

Bake for about 25 minutes, or until the top is golden brown and the crust is firm. The cake is gooey, so testing with a toothpick in the center won't tell you if it's done. Transfer to a wire rack and let cool to room temperature. Dust with powdered sugar and cut into 18 squarish pieces.

DIVINE PRAISE

We're proud of every award and accolade we've received, but being named "Top 10 Barbecue in America" by *Playboy* magazine was a novelty. Taking full advantage of this honor, one of our servers, borrowing liberally from a popular Justin Timberlake song, came up with the perfect slogan for our sign: "We're bringing sexy rack. Named Top 10 BBQ by *Playboy*."

One of our neighbors did not appreciate our humor. She called repeatedly, leaving long messages on our answering machine accusing us of promoting pornography and demanding to know when Mike Mills was going to respond to her, although she left no phone number. Each morning, we'd come in to listen to a new recording from her. She also began phoning the restaurant and passionately complaining to one of the managers. I prepared a script in response. The lucky manager who answered the next call told her we were surprised by the praise—but also concerned, since we're Christians, too. "We spoke to our minister about this, and he urged to consider this award a gift from God. National publicity is good for our town and good for our restaurant. More people coming to visit because of this publicity means we get to stay in business and employ local people."

"What did she say?" I asked.

"Well, she was silent for a moment," he told me. "Then she said, 'I want the name of that minister.'"

GIVING THANKS
AND PRAISE

WE LOVE our hometown and it sure has loved us back. The city of Murphysboro and its fine families are a huge block in the foundation upon which we built 17th Street. Mayor Will Stephens, we are grateful for your friendship and the thoughtful way you are leading Murphysboro into a brighter future.

Working side by side with our tremendous 17th Street pit crew is a pleasure and a privilege: Becky Streuter, Phillip Heern, Laurie Neef, Jenn Finney, Lisa Keller, Sammi Graff, Sandy Marks, Randy Deason, Steph Jeltsch, Chris Pritchard, and Joe Reeves, as well as our fine BOH/FOH team who help us shine on a daily basis.

Heartfelt gratitude to our brain trust: Robin Insley, ace publicist; Matt Price and Meridith Paulhus, you make us look so good; Tim Breitbach and the Coolfire Studios crew, who help us tell our story; and Jay Bennett, Sam Loccocia, Shelly and Tom Neimeier, and Ken Kellerhals, our partners in bringing to life the next phase of our dream.

The finest folks in our industry continually champion our efforts: David Knight, Elizabeth Knight Ray, Luke Ray, Andrew Bloom, Jim Compart, Marlowe Ivey, George Samaras, Derald Schultz, Primo Grills, Anders Jensen, Anne Thomsen, Weber Stephens, Shane Linn, Richard Hagmann, Wayne Lynch, Mark Lambert, Mark Kelly, Lodge Manufacturing.

Our amazing barbecue family constantly lifts us up in friendship and love—y'all are the best: John Lewis, John Stage, Jim Clancy, John Delpha, Dave Raymond, Barry Sorkin, Damon Wise, Shane McBride, the Ribdiculous boys, David Bogan, Mike Emerson, Sarah and Sam Jones, Martha Ann and Patrick Martin, Desiree Robinson, Melissa Cookston, Leslie Scott, Elaine and Garry Roark, Melzie Wilson, Carolyn Wells, Debby and Bill Gage, Chris and Mike Peters, Bob Yarmuth, Christie Schatz, Barbara Latimer, Scott Frantz, Rich Lucy, the Orrison family, Chris and Amy Lilly, Carolyn and Don McLemore, Carey Bringle, Jonathan Fox, Justin Fox, Elizabeth Moore, Anne Marie and Jimmy Hagood, Rodney Scott, Melany and Drew Robinson, Levon Wallace, Tuffy Stone, Chris Hart, Andy Husbands, Grady Foutch, John Farrish, Bob Striegel, Kathryn Twenhafel, and the late Dan Volland.

We cherish your friendship and support: Pat Daily, Tom Viertel, Danny Meyer, Michael Symon, Jeffrey Steingarten, Will Guidara, Daniel Humm, Anthony Rudolf, Aaron Ginsberg, Gerry Dawes, and Jeff Streuter.

To the hundreds of people who have traveled from all over the world to attend our OnCue Consulting classes: We revel in your success.

Special Thanks from Amy

I worked with a veritable dream team to produce this book: Ken Goodman, your photographs capture the essence of 17th Street. Thanks to Angie Mosier for leading me to Lisa Donovan, whose expert styling eye, organizational genius, and extra pair of hands were a godsend. RH Weaver, a toast to your cocktail creations and superb styling. Sala Harper, thank you for testing the desserts and baking beautiful renditions for the photo shoot. A great big hug and extra special thanks to Becky Streuter, who spent long hours assisting in the translation of our trademark recipes for home use, prepared dozens of beautiful dishes for photo shoots, and helped gather so many props. Deep appreciation to Mike Jones, director of the General John A. Logan Museum, for expert fact-checking and historical photo research.

Every writer should be so lucky as to have an agent like Janis Donnaud in their corner. She did double duty this time around and I am truly thankful for her encouragement, advice, and constant pep talks. Fathomless gratitude!

The book proposal benefited greatly from Rachel Holtzman's finesse and polish.

Miriam Harris was our outstanding editor on *Peace, Love, and Barbecue* and she patiently worked with me over a period of several years, hunkered down in the lobby of the Roger Hotel, helping me organize and craft the story arc for *Praise the Lard*. More important, she coached and collaborated and helped shape this final product, which is immensely better because of her input.

We are proud as punch to be published by Houghton Mifflin Harcourt. Rux Martin is quite simply the best in the biz—I'm eternally grateful for your devotion, ideas, enthusiasm, and expertise. The topnotch team at HMH, Melissa Lotfy, Sarah Kwak, and Jamie Selzer, deftly shepherded this book along every step of the way—I truly appreciate your patience and good cheer. No one said it would be easy, but the end result is certainly worth it.

Virginia Devlin, Shannon McGovern, Beth Schiff, and Elena Gallon—who send incredible opportunities my way. Reruns—the gift that keeps on giving!

Sam Jones, Keith Schmidt, Bryan Bracewell, Barrett Black, Tim Mikeska, LeAnn Mueller, and Wayne Mueller—who are my band of brothers in the extra special "children of legends" club.

The best friends in the world, who carry me home: Paula and Scott Maloney, Nida and Todd Mudd, Jami Gregory, Jeff Harmon, Kat Kinsman, Mitchell Davis, Nate Goldstein, Mark Dolan, David Grunfeld, Jamie Darling, and Sarah Robbins.

Family is everything. Thank you for cheering me on: Christopher Mills, Molly Hudgins and Tracey Bione, Lane and Joe Hudgins, Flo and Jem Hudgins, John Hudgins, Landess Mills, Libby Stiegman, and Chris Mills.

I felt the presence of my Mama Faye and Aunt Jeanette every single day while I was writing. Were they still here on Earth, they would have had even more input.

Above all else, my favorite job and top priority is being a mom. My children, Woody and Faye Landess, are incredibly patient with their always-working mother, and they cheerfully accompany me all over the country, proudly representing 17th Street and forming their own relationships within the food and barbecue worlds. When our first book was published, they mastered the art of stealthily remerchandising bookstore shelves, and I can't wait for them to be back at it this time around. I'm so very proud of both of you.

Special Thanks from Mike

Everything I am today I owe to Mama Faye Mills and my siblings Landess Mills, Bob Mills, Jeanette Hudgins, and Mary Pat Mills. Everything this book is today I owe to my daughter, Amy Jane: You made it all happen, from hatching the idea and landing the book deal to writing every word of the manuscript and going over every detail with me to make sure we got the story told and the recipes written properly. You sure have done me proud.

Barbecue generation: Amy's son, Woody, with Sam Jones' daughter Elaina

RESOURCES

Please visit 17bbq.com/resources to find links for many of these products. In some cases, you'll be able to learn where products are sold near you, and in others, you'll be able to order an item to be shipped to you.

SEASONINGS AND SPICES

Barry Farm

For molasses powder

Wapakoneta, Ohio
barryfarm.com and
amazon.com

Gochujang

A savory, spicy fermented Korean condiment

Available at international grocery stores, Target, or yummybazaar.com

Himalayan pink crystal salt

Large-crystal salt for holding oysters

Available at thespicelab .com and amazon.com

Townsend Spice & Supply

For cooking spices and ingredients to make rubs, sausage, and more, plus 18-mesh pepper and pickling spice

townsendspice.com
870-368-3688

CORNMEAL, GRITS, AND FLOUR

Anson Mills

Columbia, South Carolina
ansonmills.com
803-467-4122

Geechie Boy Grits

Edisto Island, South Carolina
geechieboymill.com
843-631-0077

Hagood Mills Grits

Charleston, South Carolina
foodforthesouthernsoul .com
800-538-0003

King Arthur Flour

Available at select grocery stores (check website for a store near you) and at kingarthurflour.com and amazon.com

White Lily Flour

Available at select grocery stores (check the website for a store near you) and at whitelily.com and amazon.com

SPECIALTY INGREDIENTS

Lavington Farms Cane Syrup

Charleston, South Carolina
foodforthesouthernsoul .com
800-538-0003

Poirier's Cane Syrup

Youngsville, Louisiana
realcanesyrup.com

Steen's 100% Pure Cane Syrup

Abbeville, Louisana
steensyrup.com,
cajungrocer.com, and
amazon.com
800-725-1654

Gel food coloring

In every color, for coloring cakes and cupcakes

Available at Wilton.com and amazon.com

Peg Leg Porker Tennessee Straight Bourbon

Nashville, Tennessee
peglegporker.com
615-829-6023

Rancho Gordo Beans

Dried beans for baked beans

Napa, California
ranchogordo.com
800-599-8323

Sanding and sparkling sugars

In every color, for edging cocktail glasses and decorating desserts

Available at Wilton .com. CK Products sugar available at amazon.com

Virginia Diner Peanuts

Wakefield, Virginia
virginiadiner.com
800-642-6887

PURE CANE SUGAR SODAS

Blenheim Ginger Ale

Varieties of spicy, pure cane sugar ginger ale

Hamer, South Carolina
blenheimgingerale.com
800-270-9344

Cannonborough Beverage Co.

North Charleston, South Carolina
cannonbevco.com
843-270-5072

Cheerwine

Soda with a hint of wild cherry

Salisbury, North Carolina
cheerwine.com
704-637-5881

Excel Bottling

Breese, Illinois
excelbottling.com
618-526-7159

Fitz's Root Beer Bottling Co.

Saint Louis, Missouri
fitzsrootbeer.com
314-726-9555

COOKWARE AND SERVEWARE

Boos Cutting Boards

Effingham, Illinois
johnboos.com
888-431-2667

Butterpat Cast-Iron Pans

Available at
cowboycauldron.com

Cake stands

Fishs Eddy

New York, New York
fishseddy.com
862-772-3971

Cambro

Square 16-, 18-, or 22-quart polycarbonate food containers for brining

Available at
webstaurantstore.com

Food-grade plastic buckets in 3.5- or 5-gallon sizes for brining briskets and pork bellies

By Living Whole Foods, available at amazon.com

Food-safe 5-gallon bucket liners for marinating

Available at amazon.com

Galvanized metal trays

Contact your local HVAC company or

Voss Heating and Air Conditioning

Murphysboro, Illinois
vossheating.com
618-565-0586

Igloo Coolers

Katy, Texas
igloocoolers.com
866-509-3503

Lodge Cast-Iron Pans and Cookware

South Pittsburg, Tennessee
lodgemfg.com

Pepper mills

Choose an adjustable-grind model to grind fresh pepper

Available at
williamssonoma.com and amazon.com

R. Murphy Knives

Fine carbon-steel knives

Ayer, Massachusetts
rmurphyknives.com
888-772-3481
The Legend series available at 17bbq.com

Smithey Ironware Co.

Cast-iron pans

Charleston, South Carolina
smitheyironware.com
843-619-0082

Spice mills

Multiple models available at williamssonoma.com and amazon.com

Victorinox

Fibrox pro brisket knife

Monroe, Connecticut
victorinox.com
800-442-2706

Weck Jars

Glass canning jars from Germany

Crystal Lake, Illinois
weckjars.com
800-345-7381
Also available at amazon.com

Yeti Coolers

Austin, Texas
yeti.com
512-394-9384

SAUSAGE MAKING AND MEAT GRINDING

Sugar Cure

For brining pastrami

17th Street Barbecue
17bbq.com
618-684-8902

Casings for sausage making

sausagemaker.com and
townsendspice.com

LEM Products

Meat grinders and sausage stuffers

West Chester, Ohio
lemproducts.com
877-336-5895
Also available at
townsendspice.com

BARBECUE GEAR, TOOLS, AND GADGETS

12-inch barbecue string mop

Available at
webstaurantstore.com

Gloves

Charguard Coated Heat-Resistant Gloves

String-knit gloves (to wear under nitrile or latex gloves)

Available at Uline.com

Grill Grates

Ridged aluminum grates that fit on any grill

Atlanta, Georgia
grillgrate.com
877-380-2527

Heavy-duty trigger spray bottles

A variety available at
amazon.com

Hurom HT Slow Juicer

slowjuicer.com
800-253-2140
Also available at
amazon.com

Kingsford Charcoal

kingsford.com and
available at amazon.com

Looftlighter

For lighting fires

looftlighter.com and
available at amazon.com

Meat saw

18- or 22-inch butcher hand meat saw

Available at webstaurant
.com and amazon.com

Oversized spatulas

A variety available at
amazon.com

Pink butcher paper

Oren International

Pensacola, Florida
oreninternational.com
850-433-9080
Also available at
amazon.com

Plastic squeeze bottles

For storing and dispensing sauces

Available at
webstaurantstore.com
and amazon.com

Porkinator

Tool that attaches to a drill to quickly shred pork

porkinator.com
209-232-5408

R. Murphy Knives

Fine carbon-steel knives

Ayer, Massachusetts
rmurphyknives.com
The Legend series available
at 17bbq.com

Royal Oak Charcoal

royal-oak.com and available
at amazon.com

Thermoworks

Instant-read digital thermometer and Smoke kit

thermoworks.com
800-393-6434

Victorinox

Fibrox Pro brisket knife

Monroe, Connecticut
victorinox.com
800-442-2706

PITS AND GRILLS

Austin Smoke Works

Custom fabricated steel offset wood-fired smokers from $7,500

Austin, Texas
austinsmokeworks.com

Backwoods Smoker

The Whole Hog model from $9,930

Shreveport, Louisiana
backwoods-smoker.com
318-220-0380

BQ Grills

Charcoal/wood-fired pig cookers, from $2,500 to $4,400

Elm City, North Carolina
bqgrills.com
252-236-4464

Cowboy Cauldron

From $1,695 to $2,995

cowboycauldron.com
801-918-4490

Ole Hickory Pits

*Ole Hickory Ace MM
from $5,900*

*Ole Hickory CTO-DW
from $9,500*

Cape Girardeau, Missouri
olehickorypits.com
800-223-9667

Peg Leg Porker

*Whole hog cookers from
$5,000 to $12,000*

Nashville, Tennessee
peglegporker.com
615-829-6023

Pit Barrel Cooker Co.

From $299

pitbarrelcooker.com
502-228-1222

PK Grills

From $370

Little Rock, Arkansas
pkgrills.com
866-269-8020

Primo Kamado

*A variety of sizes and
accessories from $845 to
$2,300*

Tucker, Georgia
primogrill.com
770-492-3920

Red Box Smoker

From $397

Southaven, Mississippi
ssomd.com
901-831-1451

Weber Summit Charcoal Grill

From $1,250

weber.com
800-446-1071

ORGANIZATIONS

National Barbecue Associaton

nbbqa.org

Southern Foodways Alliance

southernfoodways.org

GET THE LOOK

Dickie's

Work shirts

dickies.com

Levi's 517

Denim jeans

levis.com

Lucchese

*Amy's custom and
off-the-rack boots*

lucchese.com

Red Wing

Mike's work boots

redwing.com

Silkworm Ink

*Embroidery, silkscreening,
and customization of our
uniforms*

Murphysboro, Illinois
silkwormink.com
618-687-4077

MEAT

Big Muddy Hogs

*Premium heritage-breed Red
Wattle pork*

Hurst, Illinois
bigmuddyhogs.com
618-922-8724

Compart Family Farms

*Premium heritage-breed
Duroc pork*

compartduroc.com
877-441-2627

Heritage Farms Cheshire Pork

*Premium heritage-breed
Cheshire pork*

Seven Springs,
North Carolina
heritagecheshire.com
888-983-2494

Holy City Hogs

Heritage-breed hogs

Wadmalaw Island,
South Carolina
holycityhogs.com
843-754-0812

Newman Farm

*Premium heritage-breed
Berkshire pork*

Myrtle, Missouri
newmanfarm.com
417-938-4391

Wichita Packing Company

High-quality pork ribs

Chicago, Illinois
wichitapacking.com
312-421-0606

Certified Angus Beef

certifiedangusbeef.com
330-345-233

Snake River Farms

*American Kobe
(Wagyu) beef*

snakeriverfarms.com
877-736-0193

Island Creek Oyster Company

*Oysters from the coast of
Massachusetts*

Duxbury, Massachusetts
islandcreekoysters.com
781-934-2028

Smoky memories: Mike's father, Leon Mills

INDEX

NOTE: Page references in *italics* indicate photographs.